WA 1000584 6

£6.95

THE POLYTECHNIC OF WALES LIBRARY

Llantwit Road, Treforest, Pontypridd.
Telephone: Pontypridd 405133

Books are to be returned on or before
the last date below

This book is not available for
loan until

2 3 JAN 1987

It may be reserved by completing
a reservation card.

03. JUN 87   1 MAR 1995

2 6 MAY 1995

19. JUN 87   25 FEB

-1 MAR 1988   16 FEB

24. NOV

14. FEB 91   -5 MAY 2010

14. MAR 91

D1350855

CAMBRIDGE PAPERS IN SOCIAL ANTHROPOLOGY

EDITORIAL BOARD:

PROFESSOR MEYER FORTES, DR J. R. GOODY

DR E. R. LEACH, DR S. J. TAMBIAH

No. 2

ASPECTS OF CASTE IN SOUTH INDIA, CEYLON AND NORTH-WEST PAKISTAN

CAMBRIDGE PAPERS IN SOCIAL ANTHROPOLOGY

ASPECTS OF CASTE IN SOUTH INDIA, CEYLON AND NORTH-WEST PAKISTAN

EDITED BY

E. R. LEACH

CAMBRIDGE UNIVERSITY PRESS

CAMBRIDGE

LONDON · NEW YORK · MELBOURNE

305.5
ASP

Published by the Syndics of the Cambridge University Press
The Pitt Building, Trumpington Street, Cambridge CB2 1RP
Bentley House, 200 Euston Road, London NW1 2DB
32 East 57th Street, New York, NY 10022, USA
296 Beaconsfield Parade, Middle Park, Melbourne 3206, Australia

© Cambridge University Press 1960

ISBN 0 521 07729 X hard covers
ISBN 0 521 09664 2 paperback

First published 1960
Reprinted 1962, 1969, 1971, 1979

First printed in Great Britain at the University Press, Cambridge
Reprinted in Great Britain by
Redwood Burn Limited, Trowbridge & Esher

19.8.87

1000584 6

CONTENTS

MAPS AND DIAGRAMS

CONTRIBUTORS TO THIS ISSUE

(updated 1979)

MICHAEL BANKS. Took his Ph.D. at Cambridge in 1957 and later held a post in the Foreign Office London.

FREDRIK BARTH. A graduate of the University of Chicago who took his Ph.D. at Cambridge in 1957 and is now Professor of Anthropology in the University of Oslo. In the course of his career he has carried out field research in Norway itself, in Kurdistan, Swat, Persia, Arabia and New Guinea. He has major publications in all these areas, the most immediately relevant being *Indus and Swat Kohistan* (1956) and *Political Leadership among Swat Pathans* (1959).

KATHLEEN GOUGH. Took her Ph.D. at Cambridge in 1950. She has subsequently held teaching posts at Brandeis University, the University of Oregon and Simon Fraser University. She now resides in Vancouver where her husband David Aberle is a Professor in the University of British Columbia. She has had very extensive field experience in South India. A number of her earlier papers relating to the social anthropology of Malabar and Tanjore are listed elsewhere in this volume.

E. R. LEACH. Recently retired from the offices of Professor of Social Anthropology and Provost of King's College in Cambridge University. His principal field research was carried out in Burma, Sri Lanka, Sarawak and Kurdistan. His numerous publications include *Pul Eliya: a Village in Ceylon* (1961). He was editor of *Dialectic in Practical Religion* (1968) which was No. 5 in this series.

NUR YALMAN. Took his Ph.D. at Cambridge in 1958 where he was a bye-Fellow of Peterhouse. He subsequently held a senior post at the University of Chicago and is now a Full Professor at Harvard. He spends part of each year in his homeland Turkey. His publications include *Under the Bo Tree* (1967) which is a study of caste and kinship in the interior of Sri Lanka.

NOTE ON THE SPELLING OF CASTE NAMES

Caste names appearing in this book are romanized according to the following conventions:

Tanjore castes: as in E. Thurston, *Castes and Tribes of Southern India* (Madras, 1909).
Jaffna castes: as in J. Cartman, *Hinduism in Ceylon* (Colombo, 1957).
Kandyan castes: romanized from Sinhalese spelling.
Swat castes: as in Fredrik Barth, *Indus and Swat Kohistan: an Ethnographic Survey* (Oslo, 1956).
Some inconsistency between the Tanjore and Jaffna names is unavoidable. The following 'equivalents' may be noted:

Tanjore	*Jaffna*
Pallan	Palla
Paraiyan	Paraiyar

PREFACE

This is the second of a series of occasional papers in social anthropology published by the Cambridge University Press for the Department of Archaeology and Anthropology of the University of Cambridge. We plan to publish further volumes at intervals of about one year. Each volume will be edited by one member of the editorial board and will contain a number of papers arising out of the anthropological research work carried out in the Department. Each volume will deal, as far as possible, with a single broad topic of theoretical interest. The main contributions will ordinarily take the form of papers based on field research in particular areas and communities but each volume will also include an introductory paper in which the main theoretical issues referred to in the other papers will be explicitly discussed.

The third number of the series will use material mainly from Africa and will be concerned with problems connected with marriage. It will be edited by Professor Meyer Fortes who will also contribute the general introduction.

We are indebted to the Smuts Memorial Fund of the University of Cambridge for a grant in aid of the publication of this series. Thanks are also due to the Behavioral Sciences Division of the Ford Foundation for a personal grant to E. R. Leach which provided research assistance for the present publication.

MEYER FORTES
JACK GOODY
E. R. LEACH

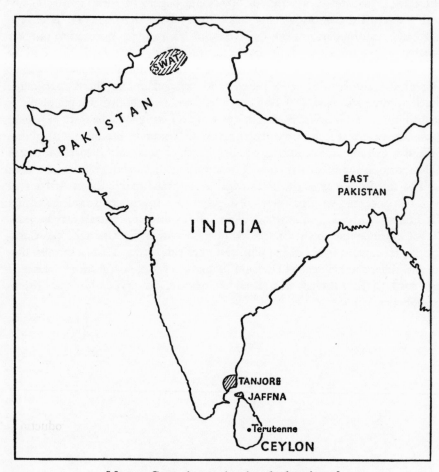

Map 1. General map showing the location of
Tanjore, Jaffna, 'Terutenne' and Swat.

INTRODUCTION: WHAT SHOULD WE MEAN BY CASTE?

By E. R. LEACH

The contributors to this symposium have in common that each has at one time or another worked in the Department of Archaeology and Anthropology at Cambridge University. They share a common viewpoint about the nature of social anthropology as an academic discipline and they share too a common interest in the cultures of the Indian sub-continent. But the essays which make up this volume, while they centre round the common theme of 'caste', have not been written from any common theoretical standpoint. Each essay stands by itself as an individual contribution to ethnographic knowledge.

Even so, taken as a collection, the essays are something rather more than a sum of individual statements on a common topic. Although each author writes of caste from a personal, individual point of view, certain interesting generalizations emerge from their joint discussions, and in this Introduction I shall try to set them out. I should stress perhaps that I am expressing a personal opinion which is not necessarily shared by any of my fellow contributors.

In the writings of anthropologists and sociologists the word 'caste' is used in two different senses. As an ethnographic category it refers exclusively to a system of social organization peculiar to Hindu India, but as a sociological category it may denote almost any kind of class structure of exceptional rigidity. Such double usage is unfortunate; the tendency to stress the 'status-group' component of caste prejudges the whole question as to what is the essential sociological nature of the Indian phenomenon. Conversely the merging of class and caste concepts is liable to lead to a highly distorted image of the nature of 'colour-bar' and other manifestations of rigid social differentiation (Cox 1948). Although the issue is approached indirectly, this ambiguity in the meaning of the word 'caste' is the central problem with which all the essays in this symposium are concerned.

In a formal sense, the word 'caste' as it occurs in this volume should always be taken to have its ethnographic Hindu meaning. The arrangement of the book is that the first, and longest, essay describes a *typical* example of caste organization in Southern India. The succeeding essays then describe variants of this pattern as they occur in Ceylon and North-west Pakistan. These variants diverge further and further from the ideal type, though each of them has been derived historically from a Hindu model. In effect the reader is invited to consider for himself just how far a social system can differ from the orthodox Hindu prototype yet still deserve the cultural label 'caste'.

Such a presentation raises directly the question as to whether caste is best considered as a cultural or as a structural phenomenon. This is an issue on which the authorities seem notably confused. Weber, for example, states categorically that 'Caste...is the fundamental institution of Hinduism' (Gerth and Mills 1947: 396). He implies thereby that caste is a specifically *cultural* concept, but then he proceeds at once to the remark that 'there are also castes among the Mohammedans of India...castes are also found among the Buddhists' (Gerth and Mills 1947: 396). This contradiction leads logically enough to an inquiry into the nature of caste, but here Weber's standpoint keeps shifting. On the one hand we are given various illustrative details of typical Hindu caste behaviour (i.e. cultural evidence) but this is backed up with a highly generalized discussion of the nature of 'closed status groups', race relations in the United States, and the behaviour of the European nobility (i.e. structural evidence). Weber thus evades the whole question as to what there is about caste which is specifically Hindu. Having started by implying that caste is peculiarly a Pan-Indian phenomenon, he proceeds immediately to the discussion of caste analogues in non-Indian contexts. Clearly he is using the word caste in an ambiguous way but he does not justify this procedure.

The same criticism may be levelled against those 'diffusionist' writers who manage to find historical examples of caste behaviour all the way from Ancient Egypt to modern Fiji (e.g. Hocart 1950; Hutton 1946: chs. IX–XI). They start by assuming that caste is definable as a list of ethnographic traits characteristic of Hindu India and then slide imperceptibly into the assumption that caste refers to certain features of social structure. Such ambiguity is no doubt difficult to avoid, but we need to be clear that it exists.

Definitions of Indian caste have usually taken the form of a list of cultural traits which are supposed to form a syndrome. The authorities, while admitting a great range of detailed variation, have mostly maintained that there is a certain minimal set of primary characteristics which together embody the real essence of caste everywhere; Hutton, for example, holds that normally caste conforms to the following criteria:

(1) A caste is endogamous.

(2) There are restrictions on commensality between members of different castes.

(3) There is a hierarchical grading of castes, the best-recognized position being that of the Brahman at the top.

(4) In various kinds of context, especially those concerned with food, sex and ritual, a member of a 'high' caste is liable to be 'polluted' by either direct or indirect contact with a member of a 'low' caste.

(5) Castes are very commonly associated with traditional occupations.

(6) A man's caste status is finally determined by the circumstances of his birth, unless he comes to be expelled from his caste for some ritual offence.

(7) The system as a whole is always focused around the prestige accorded to the Brahmans (Hutton 1946: 49 and ch. VI).

Now let us consider our specimen examples. Dr Gough's Tanjore example was explicitly intended to represent a model type. As might be expected we find that Hutton's generalizations apply in full; indeed, in her opening paragraphs, Dr Gough herself defines caste in much the same way. The fact that she refers approvingly (see below, p. 11) and without comment to that very Weberian analysis of caste which I have myself just criticized should not be taken to indicate any major difference in our points of view. It is simply that I have had the advantage of writing last!

The scene of the second essay is Jaffna, a few miles south of Tanjore across the Paik Strait. Here Dr Banks displays the same system modified. The high social status of the Brahmans and of the other ritual 'twice born' has disappeared. The dominant caste, the Vellāla, are not, ritually speaking, 'twice born' at all. Moreover, although the ideology of pollution remains intense, endogamy at the sub-caste level (*sondakara* caste) is an idea rather than a fact, and this leaves room for some degree of intercaste mobility.

For the third essay Dr Yalman takes us 150 miles still further south to the borders of the Kandyan Highlands. Here we are among Buddhist Sinhalese, who might be expected, on religious grounds, to repudiate caste altogether. In fact, although there are no Brahmans and the practical boundaries of sub-caste endogamy are even vaguer than in Jaffna, much of the 'ideology' of caste remains. Endogamy, 'pollution' and rank are ideas on which the local population lays great stress; it is only in the application of these ideas that the pattern becomes atypical. As a description of the small-scale dynamic of a caste system, Dr Yalman's analysis seems to me something of a *tour de force*. In his view, pollution ideology among the Kandyans attaches not so much to occupation and birth status as to family name and place of residence, either of which can be changed at will. He sees the caste phenomenon as the end-product of a voluntary preference for close kin group endogamy, and his essay is largely taken up with a demonstration of why such close endogamy should appear to Kandyans to be the most rational choice of action. There may be places where he overstates his case but this is certainly one of the most illuminating studies of the factors which may govern arranged marriages that I have ever encountered.

His other main emphasis is on the importance for caste systems of the ritual value of names—names of castes, names of people, names of places—and on the possible advantages of changing such names.

This somewhat novel argument deserves careful attention. Name-changing as an adjunct to changing social status is a phenomenon which we meet with in many societies but I doubt if it is anywhere more systematized than in Ceylon where the process seems to have been at work since the earliest days of European colonization. [1]

The flexibility which such practices imply might suggest that Sinhalese caste is very far removed from the Indian ideal type, but this is not really the case. So far as the Kandyan region is concerned, the typology of labour specialization and the way in which members of different castes are bound together by the obligations of ritual and economic service is entirely in accord with the orthodox Indian pattern. Despite certain peculiarities, Kandyan caste is still caste in the Indian cultural sense of the term and not simply because of a structural analogy. Hocart no doubt overstated his case when he tried to represent the Sinhalese pattern as the prototype of all Indian caste systems (Hocart 1950), but he was not being entirely foolish.

Even so, a comparison of the Jaffna and Kandyan essays brings me back to my original question. The Tamils of Jaffna are Hindus; the Sinhalese of the Kandyan hills are not. Both the Jaffna-ese and the Kandyans have caste systems which are atypical when viewed from an Indian standpoint, but the latter is not notably more aberrant than the former. The deviation of either from Dr Gough's ideal type cannot be attributed merely to the cultural frontiers of language and religion. Are there then elements in normal Indian caste organization which are essentially structural in their nature and independent of Hindu cultural origins?

Finally we come to Dr Barth's paper on the 'caste system' of Swat in North-western Pakistan. In a narrowly cultural sense the pattern here is a good deal further away from the Hindu model. In this case the valuation placed on endogamy, as expressed in pollution behaviour, is relatively low; instead the emphasis is thrown on the linkage of 'caste' with occupation and hierarchical ranking. Also, and this is a very crucial point, 'caste' membership in Swat is derived exclusively by descent from the father and not from the mother—which is the exact reverse of Southern Hindu usage.

In contrast to myself, Dr Barth takes an explicitly 'Weberian' view of caste and treats the Swat *qoum* throughout as a 'status group' rather than as a functional entity with a special distinguishing set of cultural characteristics. He says specifically, 'if the concept of caste is to be useful in sociological analysis, its definition must be based on structural criteria, and not on particular features of the Hindu philosophical scheme' (see below, p. 145). With this view I am myself only partially in agreement. Elsewhere, near the beginning of his essay, Dr Barth notes that 'Swat lies on the edge of the Indian world and partakes to a certain extent of Indian traditions' (see below, p. 115) and he notes how closely similar is the system of labour organization to that of the Hindu *jajmani* system. These similarities seem to me so fundamental that structural analogies with societies wholly outside the Indian world are liable to be seriously misleading.

Though I do not entirely agree with Dr Barth on this matter I should point out that his essay represents a highly original expansion of conventional status-group theory. He exploits the concept of *involute systems* proposed by the late Professor Nadel with marked success.

Let me then state my personal opinion. I agree with all the authors of this symposium that each of the systems described is quite properly to be regarded as a 'caste system'. They are caste systems because all of them are similar in certain very fundamental ways to the ideal pattern of Hindu caste organization of which a concrete example is provided in Dr Gough's essay. On the other hand I agree with Dr Barth that this similarity is a matter of structure rather than of culture. There is no syndrome of cultural traits which is common to all the societies concerned; each of Hutton's minimal criteria is missing from one or other of these variant systems.

But where I disagree with Dr Barth (and hence with Weber and those who have followed him) is that I do not accept the view that, because caste is a structural phenomenon, it is therefore a concept which has world-wide application. Caste, in my view, denotes a particular species of structural organization indissolubly linked with what Dumont rightly insists is a Pan-Indian civilization (Dumont 1957 (*c*)). Consequently I believe that those who apply the term to contexts wholly remote from the Indian world invariably go astray. The specific character of caste systems lies in the peculiar nature of the systemic organization itself. Let me elaborate this tautology.

Most conventional Indian ethnographies are written in a way which suggests that individual castes can usefully be considered in isolation. This is deceptive. In fact, a caste does not exist by itself. A caste can only be recognized in contrast to other castes with which its members are closely involved in a network of economic, political and ritual relationships. Furthermore, it is precisely with these intercaste relationships that we are concerned when we discuss caste as a social phenomenon. The caste society as a whole is, in Durkheim's sense, an organic system with each particular caste and subcaste filling a distinctive functional role. It is a system of labour division from which the element of competition among the workers has been largely excluded. The more conventional sociological analysis which finds an analogy between castes, status groups, and economic classes puts all the stress upon hierarchy and upon the exclusiveness of caste separation. Far more fundamental is the economic interdependence which stems from the patterning of the division of labour which is of a quite special type.

It is a characteristic of *class*-organized societies that rights of ownership are the prerogative of minority groups which form privileged élites. The capacity of the upper-class minority to 'exploit' the services of the lower-class majority is critically dependent upon the fact that the members of the underprivileged group must compete among themselves for the favours of the élite. It is the specific nature of a *caste* society that this position is reversed. Economic roles are allocated by right to closed minority groups of low social status; members of the high-status 'dominant caste', to whom the low-status groups are bound, generally form a numerical majority and must compete among themselves for the services of individual members of the lower 'castes'.

In a class system, social status and economic security go together—the higher the greater; in contrast, in a caste society, status and security are polarized. It is open to every man to become a *sannyasi* and receive the adulations of his society but only at the cost of forgoing all his social rights. Under Ceylon conditions any 'Washerman' or 'Drummer' or 'Blacksmith' or other 'low-caste' individual who wishes to go to the trouble can repudiate his caste but only at the cost of losing those economic rights which accrue automatically to members of 'low-status' groups. In a class society the 'people at the bottom' are those who have been forced there by the ruthless processes of economic competition; their counterparts in a caste society are members of some closely organized kinship group who regard it as their privileged right to carry out a task from which all other members of the total society are rigorously excluded. This is just as true of Swat as of Tanjore.

The point will be clearer perhaps if we consider its negation.

In India today, as Dr Gough's essay exemplifies, a major section of the population consists of landless labourers who stand at the bottom of the social hierarchy. These people are the victims of extreme economic insecurity and are often in violent political revolt against the formal strictures of the caste system. But their economic sufferings are not *due to* their position in the caste system. The low castes suffer economically not because they are low *castes* but because present conditions have turned them into an unemployed working-*class*. What has put them in this position is not their caste but the recent rapid increase in population, coupled with the fact that the caste rules which formerly compelled the high-status landlords to support their low-status servitors have been progressively destroyed by arbitrary acts of 'liberal' legislation extending over the past 150 years (cf. p. 30).

Everywhere in India and Ceylon today whole caste groups are tending to emerge as political factions but it is misleading to think of such behaviour as a characteristic of caste as such. If a whole caste group plays the role of a political faction by competing with other such factions for some common economic or political goal it thereby acts in defiance of caste tradition. But such change of role may not be clear either to the actors or to the anthropological observer.

If a caste group turns itself into a political faction does it then cease to be a caste? Dr Gough implies that it does (p. 44) and at the end of her essay (pp. 58–9) she cites the formation of a 'caste labour union' as one among many symptoms of caste disintegration, but Dr Yalman (p. 84) cites the formation of a 'caste welfare society' as one among many symptoms of caste resilience to changing social circumstance!

My own view is that wherever caste groups are seen to be acting as corporations in competition against like groups *of different caste*, then they are acting in defiance of caste principles. For this reason I find myself in disagreement with a part of Dr Yalman's stimulating thesis. Dr Yalman treats distinctions in grade within a single named caste as different only in degree from distinctions between separate named castes of separate traditional occupation (pp. 87, 106). It is true that the Sinhalese apply the term *jāti* to both types of grouping, but they seem to me to be different in kind. Caste ideology presupposes that the separation between different named castes is absolute and intrinsic. People of different caste are, as it were, of different species—as cat and dog. There can therefore be no possibility that they should compete for merit of the same sort. But with members of different grades of the same caste, the exact opposite is the case; the grades would not exist unless their members were constantly in competition one against the other. In this respect, grades within a single caste have the nature of social classes rather than of castes.

Thus Dr Yalman's ingenious argument that the attributes of caste apply to names and places rather than to people and that individuals can be socially mobile even when castes are not, seems to me to skirt around the central issue.

For me, caste *as distinct from either social class or caste grade* manifests itself in the external relations between caste groupings. These relations stem from the fact that *every* caste, not merely the upper élite, has its special 'privileges'. Furthermore, these external relations have a very special quality since, ideally, they exclude kinship links of all kinds. In this respect all caste systems are similar; where they differ is in the degree to which the boundaries of caste groupings coincide with boundaries of territorial grouping —this last being a variable which I shall not here discuss.

For an anthropologist interested in the comparison of kinship structures there is nothing that is peculiar to Indian caste. Internally, a caste presents itself to its members as a network of kin relationships, but this network is of no specific type. The kinship systems of caste-ordered societies vary, but all types are readily duplicated in other societies historically unconnected with the Indian world. As Morgan discovered, the formal kinship organization of the Tamils is not unlike that of the League of the Iroquois!

The kinship peculiarity of caste systems does not lie in the internal structuring of kinship, but in the total absence of kinship as a factor in extra-caste systemic organization. The cultural rules of caste behaviour establish a dichotomy in the total field of social relationships—political, economic and ritual relations are external, kinship relations are exclusively internal.

In the 'orthodox', ideal type of caste structure this distinction is quite clear, and follows directly from the three caste traits of endogamy, hierarchy and occupational specialization. All relations between persons of the same sub-caste are viewed as kin relationships, all relations between persons of different subcaste are viewed as caste relationships, and the two types of relationship are absolutely exclusive. Even where sex relations across caste boundaries are tolerated this does not entail recognition of cross-caste kinship.

But in the marginal varieties of caste described in this book the dichotomy is an idea rather than a fact. The two categories, caste relationship and kinship relationship, are conceptually separate but not, in practice, *absolutely* exclusive. In Jaffna and Kandyan Ceylon an individual cannot have kinsmen in two different castes at the same time but it does appear that in some exceptional cases an individual may start life in one caste and end up in another. In Swat, the ambiguity between caste occupation and actual occupation, coupled with a general lack of stress on affinal kinship ties, makes such personal mobility even easier. It would appear indeed that in all these societies it is precisely this inconsistency between action and idea which makes individual political action possible.

But it would be a mistake to suppose that because this flexibility occurs in admittedly 'marginal' caste systems, it is necessarily absent from caste systems of 'normal' type. We should not be led into thinking that every deviation from the ideal represents a total breakdown of the system.

In the ideal type, recognition of kinship automatically implies recognition of common caste and recognition of equal social status. Hence, since caste is immutable, social status must be immutable also. Contrariwise, any difference of specialized economic or ritual function automatically implies difference of caste and social status and this difference also is immutable. I am not satisfied that any actual society ever possessed quite this kind of rigidity; the situation described for our 'marginal' cases is much more plausible. Here the opposition between caste and kinship does not in every case unambiguously distinguish social equals from social unequals; instead the system presents itself to the individual as an unstable set of conflicting obligations which call for personal decision.

Dr Banks discusses this issue directly. He shows how individual Jaffna Tamils are subject to a conflict of loyalties. They have duties to their recognized kinsmen (*sondakara* caste); they have duties to their Vellāla overlords and patrons, and they have duties to their local neighbours independently of caste and kinship. On occasions these several obligations may all be directly contradictory. Both in Kandyan Ceylon and in Swat somewhat analogous conditions prevail so that, in all these societies, the art of politics consists in exploiting to one's own advantage these latent conflicts of personal interest.

Thus viewed, caste appears as a very much more flexible type of organization than that which it is commonly supposed to be.

Nevertheless, even though the caste systems of reality lack the absolute rigidity of the ideal type, they always remain hierarchical structures. Even where Brahmans, as such, are lacking, we find that in every case there is one or more clearly defined 'dominant caste' (Pocock 1957) the members of which are in a markedly privileged political position. In the Hindu cultural sense, the Jaffna Vellāla, the Sinhalese Goyigama and the Pakhtun and Saint castes of Swat are none of them 'twice born', but in each case the structural position of these castes corresponds to that of 'twice born' groups in an orthodox Hindu system. In any caste system the factional rivalries among members of the locally privileged caste or castes are likely to be acute, but taken together these local 'twice born' form a high-status corporation for whose benefit the whole of the rest of the system appears to be organized. This is true of all our examples.

In this respect the privilege of dominant castes appears to resemble the privilege of ruling élites everywhere, so we must distinguish.

I have already made a general distinction between caste systems and class systems on the basis of their structural organization, but the case of an aristocracy deserves special attention. There are some respects in which the characteristics of a 'hereditary aristocracy' appear deceptively close to those of a 'dominant caste'.

Like castes, aristocracies everywhere show a marked tendency towards rigorous endogamy. As with caste, the sanctions which support this rule often include a valuation which makes sexual and commensal relations with the lower classes 'polluting'. We can see this in various contemporary 'colour-bar' societies, but the principle is very general. It applied to the ruling class in nineteenth-century England and even to the *aristoi* of Plato's Republic.

Again, it is true of such hereditary aristocracies that they tend, like castes, to maintain a rigid dichotomy between kinship relations and economic relations. In nineteenth-century England, the aristocracy considered it proper to intermarry with the 'professions' but never with those engaged in 'trade'. [2] Anyone with whom an aristocrat had direct financial dealings was automatically contaminated as lower-class no matter what his financial status.

Nevertheless I must insist that the difference between an aristocracy and a dominant caste is fundamental. Aristocratic behaviour is essentially confined to a small ruling clique; it is behaviour which serves to distinguish and separate the rulers from the ruled. In contrast, in a caste system, caste behaviour is something which pervades the whole society. All castes within a given cultural area are based on common fundamental institutions (Dumont 1957(*a*): iii). Essentially the same rules apply to those at the bottom as to those at the top. Caste therefore does not simply isolate an élite; instead it defines the structural role of every sector in a total organic system. Whereas a ruling aristocracy is invariably a numerical minority, a dominant caste may be, and usually is, a majority element in the total population.

It follows that the kind of dominance asserted by individual members of an aristocracy upon individual members of the lower classes is entirely different in quality from intercaste hierarchy, even though both types of relationship are concerned with economic service and even though, in both cases, one of the parties involved is necessarily of 'higher social status' than the other.

I have commented at length upon the special qualities of intercaste relationship because the various contributors, in their treatment of this topic, seem to me particularly illuminating. They have led me to the conclusion that there is something fundamentally wrong about Kroeber's well-known definition: 'A Caste may be defined as an endogamous and hereditary subdivision of an ethnic unit occupying a position of superior or inferior rank or social esteem in comparison with other subdivisions' (Kroeber 1931). It is wrong because it puts the emphasis in the wrong place—upon endogamy and rank, and because it slurs the really crucial fact that caste is a system of interrelationship and that every caste in a caste system has its special privileges.

But the principal concern of these authors is not with definition. Each essay has its own individual merits which are both sociologically and ethnographically important. Here I must leave the reader to judge for himself.

NOTES

[1] *Ferguson's Ceylon Directory 1954* lists around 6000 'men's addresses'. These include almost everyone who has any kind of political or economic influence in the country. About 4000 of the names are those of Sinhalese but of these rather less than half are of Sinhalese style. Virtually all such true Sinhalese names indicate respectable caste status. The other Sinhalese in the *Directory* mostly have names of Portuguese form such as Perera (400), de Silva (350), Fernando (300), which give no indication of caste status. Such names have originated in the past as a function of the kind of social mobility described by Dr Yalman.

[2] 'Professions' were clergy of the Church of England, naval and military officers, barristers-at-law. In the English legal system a barrister has no direct financial dealings with his client. The practice of endogamy was less strict than the theory; wealthy brewers and bankers especially were deemed to be respectable.

CASTE IN A TANJORE VILLAGE

By E. KATHLEEN GOUGH

INTRODUCTION: HINDU CASTE

This Introduction will appear trite to all who are acquainted with caste in India. It indicates only in a very general way how far the caste system of Tanjore may be treated as typical of caste in India as a whole. An excellent statement of the common characteristics of castes was given by Weber (Gerth and Mills 1947: 397–415).

Castes in Hindu India are ranked, birth-status groups. The caste, or a subsection of it, is usually endogamous; it tends to be associated with an occupation. A caste is not a localized group, but comprises small local communities, often several miles apart. Local communities of different castes form administrative units as multi-caste villages or towns. Usually, the caste communities of the village have in the past possessed hereditary differential rights in the produce of village lands, these rights being dispensed by a dominant caste group of land managers and village administrators. In towns, caste guilds of craftsmen and traders traditionally had separate organizations.

The formal ranking of castes is defined in terms of the belief in ritual purity and pollution; rules of social distance between castes issue primarily from this belief. Whatever the origins of these rules, their codification, recording and adaptation to local circumstances have been primarily the work of the Brahmans, who from their origin in the Vēdic kingdoms of the North Indian river valleys spread throughout the sub-continent as the highest caste of religious specialists. The ubiquity of the Brahmans and their common possession of a sacred literature and a body of religious laws are apparently responsible for most of the common features of caste in the different regions.

Despite the universality of the Brahman, India cannot be said to possess a single caste system, but a number of regional systems. A comparison of regional systems is required which would permit not only generalizations covering all of them, but, more significantly, statements of concomitant variation. Regional differences are related partly to ecological variation, and partly to political history (which is itself of course influenced by ecology).

Before British rule, India comprised several independent and mutually hostile political units. Within each such unit, or within a relatively autonomous subdivision (for example a tributary kingdom), the rules governing intercaste relationships had a degree of uniformity, for they were articulated with a common body of law administered by a central authority. In Hindu kingdoms, kings were dedicated to the protection of the religious laws of castes (Hutton 1946: 81–6; Sastri 1955: 306–7). The number of castes, their laws and their mutual rank were in turn modified at different periods in accordance with state policies regarding village government, land tenure or the regulation of

Map 2. Tanjore District.

trade. In the Hindu kingdoms of South India, indeed, religious and secular law appear to have been indistinguishable. In areas of Muslim rule, the articulation of state law and Hindu religious law was more complex, but here too the regional rules of caste as promulgated by Brahman or other high-caste elders appear to have been upheld by the central administration, and the judgements of caste courts to have been ratified by local Muslim governors (Hutton 1946: 81; Majumdar, Raychaudhuri and Datta 1946: 395, 560).

Castes as named categories might extend over several kingdoms, but with few exceptions castes as organized groups did not. The exceptions were (in some areas) the Brahmans and certain trading castes, who at some periods had caste organizations extending beyond the kingdom (Sastri 1955: 318–20). For many castes, however, intra- and inter-caste relationships were confined within an administrative subdivision of the kingdom. In South India, at all events, the village itself appears generally to have been the basic unit of regular economic, social, ritual and legal co-operation between caste communities, although the endogamous group of each caste always extended over a number of villages. The village was however an almost self-sufficient unit for the production of food and many other basic necessities; it was frequently a unit of land-ownership, and it was an administrative unit within which most of the day-to-day disputes within and between caste communities were settled. Social relationships within the village, together with the relationships of each caste community to others of its wider endogamous group, with the administrative ties of the village to the government, and with its external relationships to certain trading castes, therefore comprised a large segment of the total social structure of the pre-British kingdom, although knowledge of the structure of government and of the urban caste guilds is of course necessary to complete the picture.

British pacification of the country removed barriers to social intercourse between kingdoms. But although a central government was established, castes did not become organized on an all-India basis. For the British made no consistent use of caste in the institutions which they created. Rather, they undermined the existing legal bases of caste and left the castes to work out their own salvation in the new economy and polity. This removal of the legal bases of caste has been completed in the period of Independence.

In rural areas where the pattern of subsistence has not been too greatly modified, castes have continued to function in a more or less traditional manner, and caste-based administrative bodies have persisted unofficially outside the legal institutions of the state. In such remote rural areas the village is still a fruitful unit for the study of traditional caste institutions, although these are everywhere disappearing as a result of economic change.

As their members enter the industrial economy of the modern towns, castes lose most of their traditional functions. They cease to be exclusive occupational, commensal or administrative units, lose their hereditary differential rights in the produce of village lands and their economic and ritual interdependence, and (in the case of lower castes) tend either to challenge or to disregard the rules of ritual rank. With few exceptions, however, the subcaste, or a wider group comprising several formerly endogamous regional subcastes of the same larger caste, has so far remained endogamous. The caste in urban areas has moreover acquired new characteristics. Toward the end of the last century, many of the lower castes formed reformist associations with the object of changing their customs to conform with those of the higher castes and thus of raising their rank in the ritual hierarchy. There has also been a tendency for members of the same or closely related castes to assist each other in the competition for education and urban occupations, and (particularly since universal franchise was instituted in 1951) to throw up pressure groups which compete for political power. Such modern caste-based movements, tied as they are to an expanding industrial economy and to increasingly democratic political institutions, are however so radically different from the traditional functions of caste as we know of them over the past two thousand years, that it may be questioned whether the term 'caste' can profitably be applied to them (cf. Davis 1951: 175; Srinivas 1955 (c): 1231–2).

This study examines the functions, internal organization and interrelationships of castes in one village of Tanjore District, Madras State.[1] Since this collection of essays aims at a comparison of the 'classical' syndromes of caste in several regions, rather than of its most modern urban developments, I have emphasized what is known of the village's caste structure in the late eighteenth and early nineteenth centuries. At the same time I have tried to relate modern changes in the caste structure and loss of caste functions to changes in the villagers' relations to their means of production and to the wider society. Except with regard to the general characteristics of caste already mentioned, it is not claimed that the caste system of Kumbapettai is typical of India as a whole. The precise extent of its typicality must be assessed by comparison with similar village studies in other areas (Wiser 1936; Srinivas 1955 (a); Dube 1955; Lewis and Barnouw 1956; essays by Srinivas, Cohn and Beals in Redfield and Singer 1955; Lewis 1958; Bailey 1957; Dumont 1957(a).

THE ECOLOGY OF TANJORE

Tanjore comprises the delta of the Kāvēri (see map, p. 12). The river enters the district in the north-west; it then divides into numerous tributaries which finally reach the sea. Major irrigation works were completed by the eleventh century; others were added during British rule. The deltaic soils are excellent for wet paddy cultivation, which already in 1906 occupied three-fourths of the arable land. Dry millets are alternated with the two wet paddy crops, and coconuts and garden vegetables are grown. The south-west of the district (Arantangi, Pattukkottai and the south of Mannargudi and Tanjore divisions) comprises a drier upland tract. Before British rule, it was sparsely populated by semi-independent Maravar and Kallar castes. These castes were at various times pacified by the kings of Tanjore; at others they revolted and terrorized the agriculturalists of the delta with periodic cattle raids. The tract was incorporated in Tanjore District during British rule. Irrigation works have been extended to it since 1936, thus increasing the acreage of wet paddy land.

With an area of 3259 square miles and a population of 2,979,754, Tanjore was in 1951 one of the most densely populated parts of India. The district has six municipalities and a number of small market towns and ports, but agriculture, petty trade and hand-crafts support the bulk of the population. Very little machine industry has been developed. Railways, and main roads with bus services, link the larger towns, and cart-roads, the larger villages. Tanjore's most important connexions outside the district are with Madras, two hundred miles north-north-east, Trichinopoly, thirty-five miles west, and Madura, a hundred miles south-west (Hemingway 1906: 1–12, 93–153).

HISTORICAL BACKGROUND

By the beginning of the Christian era, the Tamil Chola kingdom was established on the delta. The structure of government, the systems of irrigation and land tax, the settlement patterns of multi-caste villages and towns, the ritual supremacy of the Brahmans and their role as counsellors of the king, were established much as in later centuries. The kingdom declined in the seventh century and became feudatory first to the Pallavas of Kanjipuram and later to the Pandhyas of Madura. The Cholas regained independence in the ninth century and reached their heyday of expansion in the tenth and eleventh centuries. For brief periods, they commanded tribute from all the kingdoms south of the Tungabhadra and east of the Western Ghats, and extended their overlordship to parts of Ceylon, Burma and Malaya. In the fourteenth century Tanjore was first conquered by Muslim invaders from Delhi, and later, in 1365, became tributary to the empire of Vijayanagar. By 1534 the Chola dynasty had disappeared. The kingdom, reduced to the limits of the present district, came under the rule of the Nayaks, Telegu governors appointed from Vijayanagar. The Nayaks declared their independence of Vijayanagar in the 1620's, but Tanjore was conquered by Marātha invaders from Bijapur in 1674. Except for brief invasions by Muslim armies from South Arcot (the southernmost extension of the Moghul Empire) in the 1690's and from Mysore in 1781, the Marātha dynasty held Tanjore until its annexation by the British in 1799. The royal family was pensioned, and died out in 1855. Tanjore became a revenue district of Madras Province, and has remained so since Independence in 1947 (Hemingway 1906: 13–53; Sastri 1955: 110–40, 165–201, 253–326; Sastri 1935, 1937; Row 1883; Iyer 1928).

THE TANJORE CASTES

Today the Hindus divide themselves into three broad categories of castes: Brahman, Non-Brahman and Ādi Drāvida.

The Brahmans regard themselves as a single caste (*jāti*), but fall into many subdivisions each of which is also, in opposition to others of like order, referred to as a caste. Most numerous are the indigenous Tamil Brahmans. They received grants of land from the Chola kings and, as a result, are still settled with their lower-caste servants in separate 'Brahman villages', mostly near the main branch of the sacred Kāvēri, along the northern border of the district. The majority of Tamil Brahmans are of the Saivite or Smārtha sect. These worship both Siva and Viṣnu but regard Ṣiva as the supreme God and profess to follow the tenets of Sankara, the eighth-century Advaita philosopher. Their subdivisions, the Brahacharnams, Ashtasahāsrams, Vadamas and Vāthimas are distinguished by minor differences in the performance of Vēdic rites. Each subdivision is divided into small regional endogamous subcastes each comprising the local communities of some ten to twenty villages. A smaller number of Tamil Brahmans belong to the Vaishnavite sect of Ayyangars, who profess to worship only Viṣnu and who follow the tenets of Rāmānuja, the twelfth-century Vishishta Advaita philosopher. Ayyangars, who fall into two major subdivisions, Vadakalais (Northerners) and Tengalais (Southerners), are similarly divided into small regional endogamous subcastes located in village communities. In each Smārtha village, and also in each Saivite non-Brahman village, one or two households of an endogamous Brahman subcaste called Kurukkals act as priests in the Ṣiva temple. A comparable priestly subcaste called Bhattachars perform the same functions in the Viṣnu temples of Ayyangar and non-Brahman Vaishnavite villages.

A small group of Telegu Saivite Brahmans, who followed the Vijayanagar conquerors, are now scattered about the district and employed as household priests by the higher non-Brahman castes. Still smaller groups of Marātha, Konkanese and Gujerati Brahmans who followed the Marātha conquerors are now traders in the larger towns. Each of these foreign groups lacks internal subdivisions but is itself endogamous.

Altogether, Brahmans form about one-fifteenth of Tanjore's population, and own the bulk of the land in some nine hundred out of two thousand four hundred villages. They are wealthier and more numerous than in any other South Indian district.

Non-Brahmans form three major categories. The first of these are aristocratic castes of traditional land managers and village administrators, who in their separate 'non-Brahman villages' occupy a position of authority comparable to that of Brahmans in 'Brahman villages'. They include the Vellālas, once the royal and aristocratic caste of the Chola kingdom; the Telegu Naidus, former soldiers and government servants of the Nayaks, now concentrated in Nannilam and Negapatam; the Tamil Kallans from the south-western uplands, some of whose ancestors, in the Nayak and Marātha periods, received estates in return for military service; and a small Marātha aristocracy, concentrated chiefly in Tanjore town.

The second category of non-Brahmans comprises tenant farmers and specialized village labourers who serve the dominant Brahman and non-Brahman aristocratic castes. Chief among them are Agamudaiyans, believed once to have been house-servants of the Chola kings; Padaiyāchis, reputedly once soldiers in the early invasions of the Pallavas; Mūppanans and Kōnāns, pastoralists who are in some areas independent of higher-caste landlords; and lower subcastes of Naidus and Kallans whose ancestors followed in the wake of invasions and became absorbed as peaceful tenants in the villages of their own aristocracies. Specialist village workers, mostly of indigenous origin, include the artisan (Kammālan) caste of Blacksmiths, Carpenters, and Goldsmiths, who intermarry, Ambalakkārans (fishermen), Nādāns (toddy-tappers), Vannāns (washermen), Vanniyāns (oil-mongers), Ambattāns (barbers), Mēlakkārans (musicians and dancing-girls), Kusavans (potters), and Pūsālis (low-caste temple priests).

The third non-Brahman category comprises craftsmen and traders of the towns. They include Tamil, Kannada, Telegu and Gujerati castes of weavers; highly skilled wood-carvers, stone-carvers, goldsmiths, silversmiths and brass idol-makers who have separated themselves from the village artisan castes; and several castes of Chettis or middlemen traders in various commodities.

Ādi Drāvidas ('Original Dravidians', a modern census classification) comprise the three lowest castes of the district, now classified as Harijans by the central government. They form about one-third of the total population. Before 1843 Pallans were agricultural serfs of landlords of the dominant castes, and today are landless labourers. Paraiyans, who were also agricultural serfs, in addition beat tom-toms for non-Brahman funerals, guard cremation grounds, and remove dead cattle from the streets of landlords. The hides of these they dispose to Chakkiliyans, who make them into shoes.

None of the non-Brahman and Ādi Drāvida castes here mentioned forms a single organized group. Each, like the Brahmans, is rather a named caste-category of similar culture and occupation comprising a number of endogamous groups each in turn divided into local communities. Most of the endogamous groups are or were once regional, but some had or have specialized occupations within the broader occupational category. Within the same caste, some endogamous groups are mutually and clearly ranked, some dispute for rank, and some, which have little or no contact with each other, are not mutually ranked at all.

Table 1. *The castes of Kumbapettai*

	Caste	Traditional occupation	Date of arrival	No. of houses	No. of people
Brahman	*Brahacharnam Smārtha*	Landlord, ritual specialist	1780's	38	286
	Vadama Smārtha	Landlord, ritual specialist	1915	1	7
	Ayyangar	Landlord, ritual specialist	1940	1	11
	Kurukkal	Temple Priest	1780's	1	15
	Telegu Brahman	Household Priest for non-Brahmans	1947	1	4
'Clean' non-Brahman	1 Vellāla	Landlord	1952	1	3
	2 Kallan	Cattle-raiding tribe	1840's	7	39
	3 Padaiyāchi	Tenant farmer	1949	1	8
	4 Agamudaiyan	Tenant farmer	1860's	4	13
	5 Telegu Nāyakkan	Tenant farmer	1906	1	3
	6 Marātha	Courtier	Indefinite	2	6
	7 *Kōnān*	Cowherd	Indefinite	20	74
	8 *Pūsāli*	Village Temple Priest	1800's	4	16
	9 *Kusavan*	Potter	1800's	3	19
	10 Tacchan	Carpenter ⎫	1780's	1	3
Kammālan⎨	11 Pattan	Goldsmith ⎬Artisan	1952	1	2
	12 Kollan (Koltacchan)	Blacksmith ⎭	1949	1	2
'Polluting' non-Brahman	13 Tamil Nāyakkan	Toddy-tapper	1870's	8	39
	14 Nādān (Shanan)	Toddy-tapper	1870's	3	13
	15 Ambalakkāran	Fisherman	1880's	5	20
'Polluting'	16 Vannān	Washerman	1941	1	4
	17 *Ambattan*	Barber	1780's	2	8
	18 Kūttādi	Puppet-player, Village Temple Dancer	1890's	1	8
	19 Korava	Basket-maker, Thief	1948	1	2
Ādi Drāvida	*Dēvendra Pallan*	Landless Labourer	1780's	77	311
	Tekkatti Pallan	Landless Labourer	1860's	12	43
Outsider	20 Muslim	Native Doctor	1941	1	3
			Village Total	199	962

NOTE. The castes in italics are those included in the village establishment before 1860 (see p. 54).
The numerals in front of the names of the non-Brahman castes correspond to the numbers on Map 3.

KUMBAPETTAI: CASTE AND THE VILLAGE SITE

Kumbapettai, a 'Brahman village' in the north-west of the district, lies eight miles from Tanjore town and four from the main stream of the Kāvēri. In August 1952 its population was 962; its area, 483 acres of wet paddy land and 114 acres of dry garden and waste. The castes, with their traditional occupations, dates of arrival, numbers, and number of households, are listed in Table 1. Their spatial distribution is indicated on Map 3.

The spatial distribution of castes corresponds in large measure to their occupational specialization and mutual ritual rank. The Brahmans, as the highest caste of landlords, live segregated in their street (*agraharam*) of large, brick-and-tile houses. Pallans, the lowest caste of landless labourers, live in small mud-and-thatch shacks crowded together in two isolated hamlets, across paddy fields, outside the village proper. The non-Brahman castes, predominantly tenant farmers and specialist workers, occupy a middle position in their streets of larger thatched houses, segregated but within easy reach

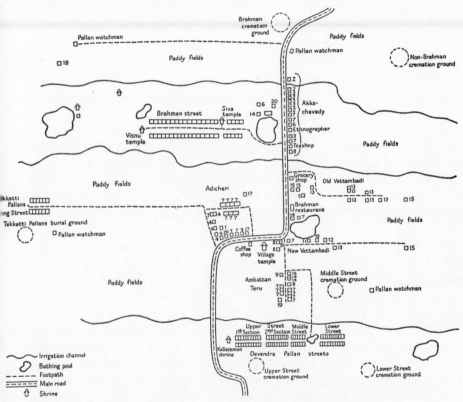

Map 3. Kumbapettai. The map is not drawn to scale.

of the Brahmans and within the main village site. The Tanjore–Kumbakonam bus-route passes through the non-Brahman area, and a few scattered non-Brahman houses, two coffee-shacks, three grocery shops and a Brahman-owned restaurant have sprung up beside it within the past twenty years. Among the non-Brahmans, caste communities are no longer strictly segregated, although some degree of caste-concentration remains. Kōnāns (cowherds) predominate in Adichēri ('serf-quarter') and Ambattān Teru ('Barbers' Street'); Kallans (former tribesmen and now traders) occupy the upper half of Akkāchāvady ('Elder Sister's Street'); two castes of former toddy-tappers (Nādāns and Tamil Nāyakkans) dominate Old Vettāmbādi ('Open Space'); and the specialist castes of Carpenters, Blacksmiths and Goldsmiths, low-caste Priests, Barbers, Washermen, and Potters tend to cluster in New Vettāmbādi near the central village temple, midway between Adichēri and Barbers' Street. The segregation of the three major caste-categories, and the partially nucleated, partially haphazard settlement of the non-Brahman castes, is explicable in terms of the historical development of their economic relationships.

CASTE IN THE TRADITIONAL ECONOMY

The present village was founded in the 1780's, after the Mysore Muslim invasion of Tanjore in 1781. Muslim armies demolished an older site, a mile to the south-west, and laid waste the surrounding paddy land. After the invasion, the Marātha Raja settled the Brahman community on its present site.

The lands then granted to the Brahmans comprised an area which today does not correspond to the social reality of Kumbapettai. Vettāmbādi and the east side of Barbers' Street were at that date unoccupied waste, and, together with the wet land east of them, belonged to the Brahman village of Nallicheri, a mile to the east. The area of Akkāchāvady was separately administered as the private estate of a Marātha concubine of the Raja, who lived there with her servants.

By 1800, the Brahmans had established in Kumbapettai a multi-caste village of a type known as the *mirāsi* village. Two other less common types of village existed (see Hemingway, 1906: 174, 191–3). One was the *inām* village, usually managed by one or more Brahman families, by the trustees of a Brahmanical temple, or by a kinsman of the Marātha royal family. *Inām* villages came into being as the result of royal grants during the Marātha period; the small royal estate in Akkāchāvady was an example of such a grant. *Inām* lands, unlike *mirāsi* lands, were partly or wholly exempt from revenue. The third type of village comprised twelve small, separately managed *zamindāri* estates on the south-western upland tract. They had been granted by Nayak Rajas to Kallan and Maravan chieftains in return for military service.

The *mirāsi* or joint village, found chiefly in Chingleput, North and South Arcot, Tanjore and Tinnevelly, was unusual elsewhere in South India, where land was normally held by separate patrilineal extended families on the *ryotwari* system of management. *Mirāsi* villages seem to have been confined chiefly to deltaic areas of the former Chola kingdom and to have arisen as royal grants of undeveloped land to village communities who undertook their irrigation (Baden-Powell, 1892: vol. III, 109–27; 1896: 362–79).

Land in *mirāsi* villages was managed jointly by a Brahman or high-caste non-Brahman community comprising some three to five patrilineal lineages each divided into several households. The village was jointly assessed for revenue twice annually by the government. Revenue was sometimes paid in cash and sometimes in kind (Hemingway 1906: 167–93). The British at first attempted to uphold the legal bases of caste in such villages, and it was not until the 1850's and later that the economic effects of British rule, coupled with certain legal changes, began seriously to modify Kumbapettai's social structure. I proceed to outline the role of caste in the village's economy between 1790 and 1860, as far as this is known. My picture of the village in this period is admittedly a reconstruction. It is derived from the villagers' knowledge of traditional institutions, some of which survive in a modified form, from documents relating to land-transfers and the organization of temples, from genealogies and from published histories of Tanjore.

The fundamental characteristic of this traditional economy was that castes were, by law, associated with specialized occupations and with differential rights to maintenance from produce in the village lands.

I have avoided the word 'feudal' because the Tanjore kingdom did not have a feudal system in the sense of a pyramidal political structure in which different orders provided service and tribute to those above them in return for rights in land. The small kingdoms of the Malabar Coast did have such a system. There, the king granted lands to hereditary chiefs, chiefs to village headmen, and village headmen to Nayar retainers, in return for tribute and military service, and within each village, lower castes had cultivation-rights in certain plots in return for services to the Nayars. Tanjore had no chiefs or village headmen, at least from the eleventh century. The government's funds were derived from land-tax collected by salaried governors of provinces, and an army of mercenaries was stationed in Tanjore town. In *mirāsi* villages the service-castes had no rights in plots of land, but only in shares in the village's grain. Both areas did however have a 'feudalistic' system in villages in the sense of ranked birth-status groups with specialized functions and hereditary, differential rights in the produce of land. The centralized state in Tanjore was appropriate to a deltaic area with a potentially high production surplus, requiring a strong central government to co-ordinate large-scale irrigation projects. The small feudal kingdoms of Malabar were appropriate to a mountainous area with a lower production surplus, reliant on rainfall for agriculture and requiring only small-scale irrigation.

In Mahratta and also early British law, all land in Brahman villages was managed jointly by the Brahman community, was impartible, and might not be sold. Kumbapettai's Brahmans comprised four exogamous patrilineal lineages of Smārtha Brahmans of the Maranad Brahacharnam subcaste, an endogamous group today distributed in eighteen villages in the north-west of the district. The system of land management is not entirely clear, but my informants thought that lands were permanently divided into a number of shares (*pangu*) of approximately equal value. Each of the four lineages controlled a fixed number of shares by hereditary right, but lands corresponding to the shares were rotated between the lineages in triennial periods. Every three years, the eldest competent man of each lineage similarly allotted a portion of the lineage's shares for usufruct to the head of each patrilineal extended family household within his lineage. Members of the same lineage were, and are still today, called *pangālis* (shareholders).

Certain fields were set aside for the upkeep of the two Brahman temples dedicated to Śiva and to Viṣṇu. A hereditary trustee managed these lands and from their produce paid a biennial stipend in grain to the temple priests. One household of Kurukkals, resident in the *agraharam*, served the Śiva temple and those of three neighbouring non-Brahman villages by hereditary right. One household of Bhattāchārs, resident in Nallichēri to the east, served the Viṣṇu temple and those of several neighbouring villages.

In return for their rights of land management, the Brahmans paid, at various periods, between forty and sixty per cent of the village's grain produce, twice annually after each harvest, as revenue to the government. Surplus paddy, not required for the villagers' consumption, was sold for cash, apparently by separate Brahman households, to merchants of the town.

The Brahmans administered their lands and the lower castes, performed religious rites within their homes, conducted agricultural and temple festivals, and periodically performed public sacrifices (*yāgams*) for the welfare of the kingdom at large. As ritual specialists, they regarded intimate participation in worldly affairs as harmful to their spiritual welfare. Religious rules prohibited them from ploughing the earth, ostensibly because this required taking the life of small insects and so was ritually polluting.

Six other castes were represented in the village in this period: Kōnāns, Pūsālis, Kusavans, Tacchans, Ambattāns and Pallans.

In the uplands of south-east Tanjore, Pudukottai, Rāmnād and Madura, where grazing grounds are extensive, Kōnāns were in some areas independent sheep- and cattle-herders, owing only a tenuous allegiance to higher castes. In the delta, where grazing ground tends to be confined within village establishments, some entered serf-like relationships with landlords of higher caste. It is possible that the Kōnāns were independent pastoralists in Kumbapettai before the village was fully irrigated and granted to the Brahmans. For the village deity is called Ūridaicchiyamman ('Kōnān mother of the village'), [2] and villagers know that at some period the Kōnāns propitiated her as a private caste deity. Later she was taken over by the Brahmans, and installed in a village temple as the patron goddess of all the castes.

Whatever their origins, about a dozen Kōnān families were settled at an early date in Adichēri as *adimai* (serfs) of the Brahmans. Each of the four Brahman lineages is said to have controlled two or more Kōnān households and distributed their services between the several households of the lineages. The right of service of a Brahman lineage was normally inherited patrilineally; many Kōnāns still know to which lineage their ancestors were attached. A serf might, however, be transferred from one lineage to another if rearrangement of numbers became desirable. Kōnān men did garden work and tended the Brahmans' cattle; women cleaned the houses of their husbands' masters, but were forbidden to enter the kitchen. Each family received materials for house-building, the use of a garden in Adichēri, the right to fish in the village bathing-pools, and gifts, including clothing, at marriages, deaths and festivals. Men were paid by their masters a fixed quantity of paddy each month; women and boys received separate smaller amounts. Like other non-Brahmans, Kōnāns further eked out their livelihood by keeping goats, chickens and cows.

The Dēvendra Pallans, whose ancestors had served the Brahmans in their previous village, were *adimai* in a stricter sense. The Kōnāns appear to have accepted serfdom from choice as an assurance of livelihood. Some communities of their caste in other areas were independent pastoralists, and if a suitable opportunity presented itself they were free to leave Kumbapettai for agricultural work elsewhere. But Pallans were by law everywhere the serfs of landlords. A truant Pallan could be returned to his master by force and, except by agreement between two landlord communities, could not change the village of his allegiance and could find no other work. Pallans were attached to Brahman households in the same manner as the Kōnāns. They received daily payments in grain and similar gifts on special occasions, but their total remuneration was less than that of Kōnāns. Their work was also more arduous, for between them men and women performed practically the whole work of grain cultivation of the village.

Four groups of village servants (*grāma tōrilālikal*) served the village at large, namely Barbers, Carpenters, Potters and Village Temple Priests. During most of the nineteenth century each was represented by a single household. These families lived on Brahman common land on the west side of Barbers' Street. Today, only one Priest's and one Potter's house remain on this site, but the street is still named after the Barbers who were its earliest occupants.

Barbers were required to shave the body hair and a portion of the head hair and to manicure the finger-nails of Brahman and non-Brahman men, twice a month, and to shave the heads of Brahman widows at similar intervals. They were also herbalists, leeches and dentists. Women of the caste were midwives for all castes above Ādi Drāvidas. Carpenters made wooden ploughs, bullock-carts, paddy-storage chests and other wooden utensils, and doors, window-frames and pillars for houses. Though they did odd jobs for all the castes, their work was overwhelmingly for Brahmans. For in this period few families other than Brahmans owned ploughs or bullock-carts, and only

Brahman houses had doors and window-frames. Even today, most non-Brahman and Pallan families live in windowless, thatched mud shacks and hang a grass mat before the doorway.

Kumbapettai Pūsālis were similarly employed primarily by Brahmans, who built and managed the village temple. Twice daily they made ritual offerings of cooked food, incense, water and flowers before the deity, sacrificed goats at festivals, provided flower-garlands for marriages, and received offerings for the goddess from Brahman and non-Brahman families after the successful birth of a child or a calf or the satisfactory conclusion of an illness.

Each of these servant groups received, as their main source of livelihood, shares from the total grain harvest of the village in February and September. Individual Barbers in addition received six measures of paddy after harvest from each man and widow in the village whom they regularly served; Priests and Carpenters received six measures from each Brahman and non-Brahman house.

The range of a village servant's clientele was in part determined by the ritual quality of his task (cf. Srinivas 1955 (b): 21–2). Hair-cutting and midwifery, like laundry work, having to do with the refuse of the body, were polluting tasks which branded the occupational groups as ritually lower than all whom they served. Non-Brahman barbers and washermen might not therefore serve Ādi Drāvidas, who ranked below them. Pallans (and also Parayans and Chakkiliyans in other villages) had their own Barbers' and Laundrymen's subcastes, one family of which served a group of villages and was paid in grain. These subcastes ranked below the majority groups of their castes and were endogamous.

Carpentry and pottery-making, although ritually evaluated as occupations, did not place the artisans in a polluting role in relation to all whom they served, for artisans were not contaminated by the refuse of their clients' persons. Ritual rules did not therefore prevent non-Brahman Potters and Carpenters from serving the Pallans, who ranked below them, and the reason why Carpenters performed few such services lay in the nature of their work, for which Pallans had little need. Pūsālis, in turn, performed few services for Pallans, not because Pūsālis' ritual work made them polluting in relation to their clients, but because Pallans were themselves so polluting to the rest of the village that they were partly excluded from its religious life. Only at the annual village festival did their leaders participate in village temple rites and receive priestly services from Pūsālis. On other religious occasions Pallans worshipped their own female deity in a caste shrine in their street.

Potters (unlike Barbers, Carpenters and Pūsālis) often undertook work for Pallans as well as non-Brahmans. For their work was both ritually neutral and also essential to the lower castes. Perhaps partly because their work was as much oriented to the lower castes as to the Brahmans, Potters, unlike other village servants, derived their maintenance in separate grain-payments from households of all the castes. Perhaps also in harmony with their numerous economic services to the Pallans, Potters had a subsidiary role as priests in the Pallan caste shrine. Their duties there were similar to the Pūsālis' role in the village temple, and they were paid twice annually by the Pallans in grain.

In addition to the separate village servant castes, four families of watchmen were drawn from the Pallan caste. Their task was to guard crops from marauding animals and alert villagers to the danger of thieves by night. Watchmen were periodically appointed by the Brahmans and lived on the common threshing-grounds. Like the castes of village specialists, they received biennial grain shares from the total harvest.

Kumbapettai drew the specialist services of Washermen, Blacksmiths and Goldsmiths from families of Mānāngōrai, the village to the south, who held hereditary rights in both villages. These families were remunerated in the same way as the Barbers, Pūsālis, Carpenters and Pallan watchmen. Washermen washed clothing for occasions such as marriages and also washed polluted cloths used during menstruation, childbirth and delivery. In addition, they provided lamps for temple festivals, decorated marriage booths and strewed cloths before funeral processions. Goldsmiths made gold and silver necklaces, ear-rings and bangles from metal provided by their patrons, and Blacksmiths made ploughshares and metal vessels. The work of all these castes was performed primarily on behalf, and under the authority, of the landlords whose villages they served. Goldsmiths and Blacksmiths formed with Carpenters a single endogamous caste called Kammālan. Kumbapettai Carpenters traditionally intermarried with Mānāngōrai Blacksmiths and, in 1947, a brother-in-law of the present Carpenter family finally moved to Kumbapettai and was given the exclusive right of the village's patronage. Similarly, in 1946, the patronage of Mānāngōrai and Kumbapettai was divided between two branches of the Mānāngōrai Washerman's family, one household of which moved to Kumbapettai as its servants.

Two other specialist castes served Kumbapettai by hereditary right. One was the non-Brahman caste of Mēlakkārans, whose men were musicians in Brahmanical and village temples. Some of the women were dedicated as temple dancers and incidentally became prostitutes for Brahmans and the higher non-Brahman castes. A community of Mēlakkārans lived in the bazaar town three miles from Kumbapettai and comprised seven patrilineal groups of musicians and dancers, each group holding the right of service in three neighbouring villages. Kumbapettai's group visited and still visits the village for Brahman marriages and temple festivals. At festivals, the players were traditionally paid in grain from the Brahman temple lands; at marriages, in grain provided by the host family.

Finally, two households of Mānāngōrai Paraiyans, the lowest Ādi Drāvida caste, served all castes of Kumbapettai by hereditary right. Their tasks were to provide wood and cow-dung for cremations, guard bodies burning in the cremation grounds, beat tom-toms for non-Brahman and Pallan funerals, and dispose of the corpses of animals. Serving as they did all castes equally on sporadic occasions, they were paid separately in grain by each household.

I have so far described the traditional occupations of the castes in which they were legally obliged, and had the legal right, to engage when required. It is clear however that even a stable, non-expanding village economy could not function entirely through the medium of hereditary, caste-determined occupations and economic relationships. Strains in the system were most likely to occur in the case of the specialist castes. A given village could not be guaranteed to provide an exactly correct demand for the services of all the barbers, washermen, carpenters, etc., who happened to be born into it. Situations of variable supply and demand appear to have been met by three main forms of flexibility. First, although rights of service in a given village or group of villages were in theory patrilineally inherited, considerable movement of specialist families took place between villages by mutual agreement between the specialists and their landlords. The supply of workers over a given region was thus kept relatively even. Second, whole caste communities might, over time, change their occupations to meet current and local demands; the Kōnāns' change from pastoralism to mixed garden work and cowherding is a case in point. Third, for the non-Brahman specialist castes, agriculture provided a secondary source of livelihood. Unemployed specialists were supplied with wet land on an annual tenure called *kuthakai* for which they paid a fixed rent in grain to the landlords, usually amounting to between three-quarters and four-fifths of the crop. Such tenures were *not* granted to Ādi Drāvidas: Pallans and Paraiyans alike were mostly serfs to landlords (p. 23) and families of Paraiyan funeral-servants who became unemployed reverted to the role of serfs. In villages where there was a large caste group of cultivators (Agamudaiyans, Mūppans or Padaiyāchis) in addition to the landlord community, such cultivators were regular tenants, and tenancy relationships tended to be hereditary. Thus in Kumbapettai, as the Kōnāns expanded, some Kōnān families became long-term tenants of Brahman households. For the specialist castes, however, *kuthakai* was a temporary expedient resorted to when their craft was not required.

The economic relationships of the castes so far enumerated had the following characteristics. Each caste group was virtually homogeneous in occupation and wealth, Brahmans being considerably wealthier than their non-Brahman servants, and non-Brahmans slightly wealthier than Ādi Drāvidas. The overwhelming majority of economic relationships were hereditary and caste-determined. In spite of the proliferation of castes, specialization was simple from an economic point of view. In most cases, different specialist groups did not co-operate in the production of a single object. Notable exceptions were the house, the plough and the bullock-cart, and it is significant that carpenters and iron-workers, whose tasks were most often complementary, formed a single endogamous group. Otherwise, specialization within the caste, except on the basis of sex and age, was almost unknown. A single household, and in some cases a single worker, could control each of such skills as cultivation, cattle-tending, pottery-making, laundry work and barbering. For most tasks the individual or the household was the labour-unit, and when the co-operation of several households or of a whole caste group was required, as in transplanting, harvesting, channel-digging or road-mending, the work tended to be uniform rather than internally specialized. Economic relationships were overwhelmingly between separate households of different castes and were dyadic: Cowherds, Agricultural Serfs, Barbers and Washermen were not involved in each other's relationships with landlords. Within the village, apparently, all economic relationships consisted of the provision of goods and services in direct exchange for paddy, the chief source of livelihood. Within the village there was no middleman trader, no market, and very little economic competition. Because the highest caste controlled all the land, the most important economic relationships consisted of the rendering of goods and services by lower-caste households upwards to one or more Brahman households in return for food, clothing and shelter. Subsidiary economic transactions took place between households of each of the specialist castes, between each of them and the Kōnāns, and between some of them and the Ādi Drāvidas, but because these transactions were dyadic and mutually separate, they did not provide a basis for co-operative bargaining on the part of blocks of lower castes in relation to the landlords. Collective opposition between the individual lower-caste group and the Brahman group was again mitigated by the strong, long-term ties of economic interest between separate households of the two castes, as well as being contained within a body of law administered by the Brahmans and supported by the central authority of the kingdom.

The simplicity of specialization, the dyadic, hereditary, inter-household nature of economic ties, the direct exchange of goods and services for subsistence, and the lack of markets and cash transactions within the village, depended on the fact that the village was an almost self-sufficient productive unit, deriving most of the basic necessities of living from its lands.

Kumbapettai did, however, engage in a variety of non-hereditary economic transactions, with unfixed prices, with castes from outside the village. These were of two types. The first type comprised simple barter relationships; groups of such itinerant castes as Basket-makers, Puppet-players and Acrobats visited the village and exchanged their wares or services for grain from

27

whoever cared to pay them. The second type comprised a variety of cash transactions, in marketing conditions, through contractual relationships, with castes of traders and craftsmen of the towns. Three circumstances appear to have prevented such cash transactions from upsetting the occupational and wealth distribution and the hereditary status relationships of village castes. First, among villagers the use of cash seems to have been almost or entirely confined to the dominant caste; it seems probable that transactions within the village and with service-castes of nearby villages were carried out entirely by barter or with grain as the medium of exchange. Second, land was not a freely marketable commodity. Dominant castes did not own land outright as a private commodity, but owned hereditary rights in its management and in a share of its produce, and these rights were not readily transferable. In 'non-Brahman' villages, more than one caste community might manage the land, but the sale of land-rights was limited to communities of the aristocratic non-Brahman castes. In Brahman villages, rights of land-management might not be sold at all to persons of other castes. Traders were thus prevented from obtaining stakes in the ownership of village resources, so that the self-sufficiency of the village as a food-producing unit was not disturbed. Third, cash trade with the towns was confined almost entirely to luxury articles. In Kumbapettai, cotton cloth appears to have been the only significant trade-article which filtered down to the lower castes, and this was distributed to them in limited quantities by the Brahmans as gifts at festivals. Within villages, sumptuary laws, defined in religious terms and sanctioned by royal authority, confined the use of such luxury items as silk clothing, most kinds of gold jewelry, brick-and-tile houses, metal household idols, carved house-pillars, and certain kinds of metal vessels, to the dominant landlord castes, and so buttressed asymmetrical status relationships between them and the lower castes.

CASTE IN THE MODERN ECONOMY

During British rule a series of interconnected legal and economic changes undermined the role of caste in the village economy. In Kumbapettai, the effects of these changes became significant during the 1860's; the speed of change and the loss of caste functions have been accelerated during this century.

In Tanjore, the following appear to have been the most significant changes during British rule:

(1) Beginning in 1800, the country was pacified and migration between kingdoms made possible.

(2) The British established a new bureaucratic political system, service in which was not intrinsically limited by caste membership. Educational institutions, related to the new political system, also provided new caste-free occupations.

(3) Intercaste service-relationships in villages were modified by the abolition of serfdom in 1843.

(4) The expansion of trade and the development of new industries provided further opportunities for caste-free employment. The opening of the Suez Canal in 1869 and the introduction of steam-powered machinery in the 1860's were significant events in this process.

(5) The introduction of railways in the 1860's made possible rapid transport and increased spatial mobility.

(6) The new occupational pursuits and consequent wealth-heterogeneity among the land-holding castes, coupled with increased trade, necessitated the break-up of jointly managed village estates and their distribution between separate patrilineal extended families of the dominant castes. This change was codified in the revenue settlement of 1865. About this time, the rights of land managers became interpreted as private land ownership, and land became a freely marketable commodity available for purchase by persons of any caste.

(7) As a result partly of natural increase and partly of immigration from less fertile districts into the delta, the population of Tanjore increased from 1,973,731 to 2,979,754 between 1871 and 1951.

In addition to changing the economic relationships between the castes already present, various combinations of the above factors brought representatives of fifteen new castes into the village after 1860.

The first significant local events which led to this influx of new caste-groups were the extinction of the royal lineage in 1855 and the subsequent break-up of the royal estates. In the 1860's, Akkāchāvady was parcelled out and bought by Kumbapettai Brahmans, Muslim and Hindu traders of the town three miles away, and a few formerly landless local non-Brahman families. Shortly after this date, Vettāmbādi and the east side of Barbers' Street were sold by impoverished Brahmans of Nallicheri, the village to the east. These areas too became occupied by new non-Brahman families, either as small cultivating landowners or as tenants of Kumbapettai Brahmans or of new landowners outside the village. The new families entered into economic relationships of one or another kind with Kumbapettai's population, although only some of them entered service-relationships with the Brahmans. As a social unit Kumbapettai thus expanded, but the economic control of the Brahmans over the lower castes was diminished.

Three types of circumstances brought new caste communities into the village. First, representatives of three castes (Kallans, Tamil Nāyakkans and Nādāns) came to Kumbapettai to trade. The Kallans, once cattle-raiders of the south-western uplands, came to buy paddy from Kumbapettai's owners and transport it for resale in the deficit areas of Pattukottai and Ramnad. The Kallans, like the Marāthas of Akkāchāvady, were already settled as bodyguards on the Marātha royal estate before 1860. When this area was incorporated in Kumbapettai they changed their occupations and became part of the village community. With the establishment of a mechanized rice mill in the nearby bazaar town in the 1930's, some Kallans became regular brokers receiving surplus paddy from Kumbapettai's owners and selling it to millowners for resale as husked rice.

Tamil Nāyakkans and Nādāns were formerly separate castes of coconut growers and toddy-tappers. In the late nineteenth century, their servicerights in villages were abolished and toddy became a marketable commodity available for sale only in licensed liquor shops. Kumbapettai's Nāyakkan family obtained a shop in Mānāngōrai and, as their wealth increased, bought plots of land in Vettāmbādi. With the introduction of prohibition in 1947, they became small owner-cultivators, tenant farmers and in some cases coolielabourers for local landowners. The Nādāns, who formerly worked for the Nāyakkans as toddy-procurers, similarly became tenant farmers in 1947.

The second category of immigrants came as a result of the modern change from hereditary, inter-household service-relationships to short-term contractual relationships between landowners and tenant farmers, village specialists and landless labourers. With the abolition of serfdom in 1843, most of the serfs became *pannaiyals* (tied labourers) of their former masters. The *pannaiyal*'s work and payments remained the same as in previous centuries, but the relationship was in theory contractual. In fact, however, the *pannaiyal* lost security and also failed to gain freedom. As trade increased and the lower castes began to require cash for private transactions in the towns, landlords made periodic cash loans to their *pannaiyals*. In this way the *pannaiyal* became tied to his master by debt rather than (as formerly) by hereditary right. He could not leave his master unless the debt was paid by a new one. On the other hand, a landlord who was willing to forgo his small loans might, under the new law, dismiss and evict unwanted *pannaiyals*. The increased power of the landlord became evident in Kumbapettai in the 1860's, when a group of Pallans serving one of the four Brahman lineages are said to have 'quarrelled' with their masters and demanded higher pay. The Brahman lineage responded by evicting them and replacing them with a new group of Pallans of the Tekkatti (Southern) Pallan subcaste, whom they brought from a Brahman village in Kumbakōnam and settled in the modern 'Long Street'. The old servants, unable to find work elsewhere, pleaded for mercy and were later re-employed.

As land changed hands more frequently, *pannaiyal* relationships became increasingly brief. Today, *pannaiyals* are engaged by the year and, although some continue to work for the same master over longer periods, many change hands every year. Further, as the labouring population increased, large numbers of landless labourers in every village each year found themselves excluded from tied labourer-relationships and forced into sporadic 'coolie' work as day-labourers paid solely in cash. Some, slightly more fortunate, were able to lease land annually on *kuthakai* tenure, often from landlords who were absent in urban work. As a result of this breakdown of hereditary inter-household service-relationships and insecurity of employment, many single families became detached from their local communities and wandered into strange villages in search of work. As a relatively sparsely populated village in a fertile area of the delta, Kumbapettai has absorbed several such stray families during the past hundred years. Pallans of the Dēvendra sub-caste joined their caste-mates in the Palla Chēri, and Agamudaiyans, Padaiyā-chis, Vellālas and Telegu Nāyakkans settled on vacant lots in the non-Brahman streets. In addition to these castes, whose work was always agricultural, stray families of Kūttādis (wandering puppet-players), Marāthas (house servants of royalty) and Ambalakkārans (inland fishermen), having left their caste-communities and traditional occupations, acquired agricultural work in Kumbapettai.

Also in the position of castes who have lost their service-relationships and entered contractual work are two families of village specialists: Telegu Brahmans and Goldsmiths. Telegu Brahmans traditionally held service-rights as household priests (*purohits*) of Naidu and Marātha aristocrats. With the extinction of the royal family and the subsequent impoverishment of its courtiers, many entered contractual work for the lower non-Brahman tenant castes who, in their efforts to rise in the ritual hierarchy, were glad to employ impoverished Brahmans as household priests. Kumbapettai's *purohit* rented a house in the Brahman street in 1947 and ekes out a livelihood by conducting marriage, funeral and ancestral rites for those non-Brahman families of the village who care to pay his fee. The Goldsmiths, having lost their service-right in a Trichinopoly village, wandered to Kumbapettai and began to do small cash jobs for local Brahmans and non-Brahmans. The Mānāngōrai Goldsmith, whose hereditary service-right extends to Kumba-pettai and who was hitherto paid annually in grain, was powerless to prevent this encroachment. For the law of the state no longer upholds his hereditary right, and the new Goldsmith, being of a different regional subcaste, cannot be disciplined by the local community of artisans.

The third category of immigrants are government servants, posted to Kumbapettai to work. They include the present village clerk, an Ayyangar Brahman, the former village clerk, a Smārtha Brahman of the Vadama sub-caste, who recently retired on a pension, and one household of a low non-Brahman caste named Korava, formerly wandering gypsies engaged in basket-making, palmistry and theft. In an attempt to rehabilitate this caste, the government recently settled several families as road-sweepers in villages. All of these families derive their maintenance in cash from government sources outside the village, have few economic transactions within it, and are in part excluded from its social life.

In general, the role of caste in the economy has undergone the following changes. First, the caste community is no longer homogeneous in occupation and wealth, for caste is today a limiting rather than a determining factor in the choice of occupation. Exactly half of Kumbapettai's adult Brahmans are now employed in towns as government servants, school teachers or restaurant workers. Of the remainder, some own up to thirty acres of land, others as little as three. One runs a grocery store and one a vegetarian restaurant. Among the non-Brahmans, the Fishermen, Toddy-tappers, Marāthas, Kallans, Koravas and Kūttādis have abandoned their traditional work. Today, all the non-Brahman castes except Potters, Village Temple Priests, Smiths, Washermen and Barbers (who, in whole or in part, retain their traditional work) and the Koravas who are government servants, are predominantly dependent on agriculture or horticulture. Irrespective of caste, however, thirteen out of fifty-six men of these castes are now paddy-traders, shop-keepers, or wage-workers in a cigar factory in the town. Among the forty-three non-Brahmans who remain in agriculture or horticulture, the mode of employment varies in a manner not determined by caste. Three are small owner-cultivators, nine are *pannaiyals* contracted by the year, ten are daily coolies, and twenty-one lease land on *kuthakai* tenure.

The Pallans have, without exception, remained in agricultural work. Whereas all were formerly landless, tied labourers, however, today only twenty-two per cent (eighteen out of eighty-four) are *pannaiyals*. Thirty-eight per cent have in the past ten years become *kuthakai* tenants on the same terms as non-Brahmans, while thirty-nine per cent have sunk to being daily coolies, and one man has risen to the status of a small owner-cultivator.

Second, castes are obviously no longer characterized by hereditary differential rights in the produce of village lands. The Brahmans are still overwhelmingly Kumbapettai's dominant land-owning group. In the modern village they own sixty-eight per cent of the wet land and sixty-one per cent of the dry. But the rest is distributed between Hindu and Muslim trading castes of the town, Brahman and non-Brahman landlords from other villages, and (in very small plots) local non-Brahman and Pallan households. The village specialist castes of Temple Priests, Barbers, Washermen and the Pallan Watchmen retain hereditary rights of service by common consent and are still paid biennially in grain, but their right is not upheld by law and the landlords may dismiss them if they wish. The traditional Barbers were in fact dismissed twenty-five years ago after a dispute with the Brahmans, and replaced by an alien, unemployed Barber who had newly returned to Tanjore from plantation work in Burma. Other specialist castes—the Carpenters, Blacksmiths, Goldsmiths and Potters—are now employed only by private contract in return for cash payments and no longer claim shares in the harvest of the village's grain. Similarly, as we have seen, Tenant-Farmers, Cowherds and former Agricultural Serfs, although still (in the case of *pannaiyals*) paid partly in grain, depend upon contractual work for their livelihood and have lost their hereditary rights.

Also significant are changes in the directions taken by economic relationships. Today, only sixty-three per cent of non-Brahmans and seventy per cent of Pallans regularly serve the Brahmans as tenants, specialists, *pannaiyals* or daily coolies. Of the remainder, some agriculturalists (both Pallan and non-Brahman) work for Muslim or Chetti landlords outside the village; a few Pallans work for non-Brahman cultivators within the village; and a few non-Brahmans work for persons of their own or a similar caste. Among the Brahmans, too, some of the smaller owners now take on *kuthakai* tenure, from their own absent kinsmen, land which they in turn give for cultivation to servants of the lower castes.

With the extension of cash purchasing power to the lower castes and the introduction of markets into the village, many economic transactions now bear little or no relationship to caste. Persons of any caste who can afford it attend cinemas and buy clothing, food and household goods from shops in the town. Within the village, grocery-shopkeepers, paddy-traders, milk vendors, potters, carpenters, blacksmiths and goldsmiths carry out cash transactions with persons of any caste from their own or other villages. The sale of cattle, ploughs, bullock-carts and even land takes place in marketing conditions which may sometimes be limited but are never wholly determined by caste loyalties. Rules of ritual pollution limit the sale of cooked food, but even here only the extremes of the hierarchy are affected. Only Ādi Drāvidas are excluded from the Brahman vegetarian restaurant, and only Brahmans refuse to enter the non-Brahman coffee-shops.

Caste is, nevertheless, still a limiting factor in Kumbapettai's economy. First, differences in average wealth, ownership of resources, education and occupational opportunities, although no longer upheld by law, persist as a legacy from the past. They seem likely to persist until greater industrial expansion offers new opportunities for livelihood to the lower castes, or until land is redistributed by the government. The Brahmans still own two-thirds of the land, and their comparative wealth and traditions of scholarship are likely for some time to give them advantages over the lower castes in the competition for white-collar employment. Similarly, non-Brahmans, on average, own more land and are slightly better educated than Ādi Drāvidas.

Second, ritual rules of caste as well as economic expediency still limit the choice of occupations in Kumbapettai. No one has undertaken forms of work or economic relationships traditionally proper to castes he considers

33

lower than his own. Several impoverished Brahmans have become waiters in vegetarian restaurants, but all have refused to plough the land. Several non-Brahmans of the agricultural castes have accepted the least profitable form of agricultural employment as daily coolies, but none would attempt to enter the polluting tasks of barbering, washing, fishing or butchering as a full-time occupation. It is noteworthy, again, that in the complex modern network of service- and tenure-relationships, no one leases land from, or serves as a labourer, a member of a caste ritually lower than his own. Further, village specialists in relatively 'clean' occupations (Kurukkals, Village Temple Priests, Smiths and Potters), when they could not find more rewarding and socially esteemed work outside their specialty, have retained their occupations and refrained from teaching them to others. Conversely, although one Kumbapettai Pallan has become a small owner-cultivator, and one Barber left the village to become a shopkeeper and a landowner of considerable means, no Brahman or non-Brahman of the village would employ members of either caste as house servants. The net result of all these caste limitations has been that whereas persons of many castes have entered modern caste-free occupations which they consider appropriate to their ritual status, except for land-ownership (now available to all who can afford it) and the various forms of agricultural work (now available to all except Brahmans), no person has changed from one *traditional* occupation to another.

THE CASTE AS A CORPORATE GROUP

Each of the larger caste communities was traditionally a localized unit with kinship, social, economic, religious and administrative functions. 'Specialist' castes, commonly represented by only one patrilineal group in each village, had an administrative unit comprising six or eight patrilineal groups distributed in nearby villages. This unit had similar characteristics to the communities of the larger castes, except that it was not localized.

In Kumbapettai in 1952, the caste communities of the Brahmans and Ādi Drāvidas retained many of their traditional functions, but those of the non-Brahman castes did not. I describe briefly the structure and functions of these communities.

1. *The Brahmans*

The Brahman street formerly contained households of the Maranād Brahacharnam subcaste of Smārtha Brahmans, and one Kurukkal family. The Kurukkals have their own organization among families of their endogamous subcaste in neighbouring villages. Today, immigrant families of Ayyangar, Vadama and Telegu Brahmans occupy rented houses in the street. These maintain kinship ties with other families of their subcastes elsewhere, but no longer participate in the administrative organizations of their natal villages. They play a modest role in the social and religious life of the *agraharam* but are excluded from its kinship, economic and administrative functions.

The Maranād Brahacharnams still form a corporate community. Six households, and a total of one hundred and thirty-four persons, are partially absent in urban work, but they return for harvests, household rites and village festivals and are consulted in major undertakings. Fifty-śix adult men, with their families, remain permanently in the village and dominate its social life.

This Brahman community comprises four dominant exogamous patrilineal lineages together with a few related households which have arrived from other villages within the past hundred years. All Brahmans of the community are related to each other by patrilineal, affinal or cognatic ties.

The Brahmans exhibit a high degree of internal interaction and external exclusiveness. As kinsfolk, they invite each other to feasts of boys' initiations, marriage, death and ancestral rites, and informal interdining goes on among friends and close relatives. The community owns in common the site on which its street is built, two temples, a bathing-pool and a cremation ground, from the use of which other castes are excluded. Houses are built with walls adjoining; holes in the walls permit women to pass messages to each other. Children are socialized within the street, and until the age of five do not mingle with those of other castes. Women know only the main road of the village outside their street and have never visited the side-streets of non-Brahmans, never seen the settlements of Pallans. Social distance between Brahmans and the lower castes is phrased in terms of rules of ritual pollution, referred to subsequently. Distance is also created by differences in the culture of Brahmans and the lower castes. The Brahmans have a different kinship system from the non-Brahmans and Ādi Drāvidas, with a different terminological structure. As carriers of Sanskrit religion and culture they, far more than other castes, possess knowledge of Puranic mythology. They alone know the Vēdic rites and hymns used in household ceremonies, and in this village they alone are vegetarians and engage in ascetic religious pursuits.

The spatial distribution of the Brahmans (and in other villages, of other landowning communities) in a compact street of adjoining houses is related partly to their ecology and partly to the former system of land management. First, the delta is predominantly an area of wet rice lands. The dry garden lands of villages form isolated small islands at wide intervals amid the vast expanse of fields. Housing is therefore bound to be nucleated, and given the ritual distance between castes, it follows that they should reside in compact caste communities. Second, the Brahmans formerly controlled in common all the village lands. It was therefore convenient for them to live together so that frequent meetings of household heads might take place to arrange such matters as the control of irrigation water, the co-ordination of agricultural activities and the allocation of lands and servants. Even today, when land is owned by separate patrilineal families, the system of irrigation requires owners to be in frequent contact to arrange such matters as the release of water from one set of channels to another during the ploughing and sowing seasons. The situation is quite otherwise, for example, in an area like the Malabar Coast, where the terrain is hilly, garden land is plentiful, and reliance on rain for wet rice lands rather than on large-scale irrigation projects permits the separate administration of small estates. There, each landowning household tends to occupy a large garden, sometimes with houses of its own lower-caste servants built near it at convenient distances.

In the late Marātha period the heads of the four Brahman lineages formed a group (*panchāyat*) responsible to the government for the village's administration and the collection of revenue. Their duties included the periodic allocation of lands and servants to separate households, the common control of the village specialist castes, and the organization of Pallans for such joint tasks as the digging out of irrigation channels before the sowing season and occasional forced labour on government projects such as irrigation works and road-building. The *panchāyat* was also concerned with the administration of justice among the Brahmans and within the village as a whole.

In 1816, the office of village headman with police and judicial functions was created by the British, and in 1836 the collection of revenue was added to his duties. Although in theory the administrative head of the village, the Brahman village headman in fact operated for several decades as merely one member of the (now unofficial) *panchāyat*. With the divisions of the village lands in 1865, the *panchāyat* lost its functions of land-allocation, but it persisted as an administrative body until the close of the century. During this century, the increasing heterogeneity of land-wealth and power among the Brahman households, and the entry of new households of alien lineages, have led to the collapse of the lineage heads' *panchāyat*. Today, the village headman has legal authority to try cases of debt, theft or other disputes involving not more than fifty rupees. His post is much sought after by young and middle-aged men of the more prominent families and is the occasion of factional disputes between the two largest lineages, who in different contexts draw to themselves the support of different related households. As one of a group of Brahmans of equal rank, however, the headman is powerless to settle disputes among the Brahmans or to govern the village at large. Instead, the heads of all the Brahman houses have, in the past fifty to sixty years, tended to meet periodically in informal assemblages to fix dates for agricultural operations such as first ploughing, transplanting and harvest, to organize lower-caste labour, to appoint the Pallan watchmen, to adjudicate in major disputes between the lower castes, and to settle general questions of village policy. [3] The assembly has no formal leader, but tends to be led at different times by one or other of half-a-dozen ambitious middle-aged men who own more land than the remainder.

Early in the century, the assembly had the power to excommunicate from caste Brahmans detected in grave offences against religious law such as fornication with Ādi Drāvidas, adultery within the caste, or interdining with lower-caste persons. The last case occurred twenty-five years ago when a Brahman was forced to leave the village after having sex relations with a Pallan woman. But in recent years no formal attempt has been made to curb such offenders. For with the widening range of economic relationships and the ease of mobility between village and town, Brahman households are economically and socially less interdependent and less bound by religious law.

Similarly, no public assembly of the Brahmans today has authority to settle disputes among them by force. Disputes concerning land, irrigation rights, slander, inheritance, debt or theft can at best be arbitrated by a third neutral party with the consent of the disputants. In extreme cases such disputes now go to the urban court.

It seems probable that even in the past the Brahmans have had less need for a formal administrative body to settle their own disputes than had the lower castes. Within each of the castes, cross-cutting ties of kinship help to prevent serious breaches of the peace. In a major dispute, the whole patrilineal groups of the disputants may temporarily become involved, but in a short time, affinal and matrilateral ties between their members serve to mitigate the group-conflict. This process is similar in all the castes, but mechanisms for the actual settlement of disputes vary. Among the lower castes, a strong organization for the speedy settlement of disputes is necessary because quarrels leading to a breach of the peace are dealt with by the Brahmans in the form of a collective punishment imposed on the lower-caste group as a whole. Being themselves the administrators, the Brahmans have no authority above them which threatens them with collective punishment if their own disputes go unsettled. Second, the fact that they are the administrators is itself a source of unity among the Brahmans. However acrimonious their own disputes may be, they are constantly forced to unite against potential offenders in the lower castes. Brahman disputes therefore tend to be less violent and more prolonged than do those in the lower castes: a modicum of unity and dignity needs to be preserved to carry on village administration, but there are few pressures toward immediate and final settlement of differences. The child-training and ideals of Brahmans harmonize with the needs engendered by their position in the caste hierarchy. The expression of physical aggression in any form against seniors or peers is considered a grave sin and evokes much guilt, whereas physical aggression may be vented upon subordinates of the lower castes. Disputes between Brahmans are

37

therefore very seldom accompanied by blows, but tend to drag on in the form of covert backbiting, mutual silence, and withdrawal into fantasies of persecution or of secret revenge. Among the lower castes, physical violence toward persons of higher caste is necessarily strictly inhibited, but tends to be readily vented upon peers within the caste. The lower castes tend therefore to be characterized by periodic sullen resentment against superiors of higher caste, coupled with violent but speedily terminated disputes between peers.

As religious specialists, the Brahmans are much concerned with the collective performance of religious rites. The community owns two temples (built one at either end of the street) dedicated to the Sanskrit gods Śiva and his consort Parvati, and Viṣnu and his consort Lakshmi. Each deity owns a portion of wet land, the incomes from which are managed by a hereditary Brahman trustee and used to pay the temple priests and to finance daily rites. Since the Temple Entry Act of 1947, the lower castes have been theoretically free to attend these temples, but none do so in fact. Eight major festivals are conducted each year in one or other temple; portions of each of these are financed in turn by minor segments of the Brahman lineages. The Puranic myths associated with these festivals, in which the Brahmans are deeply interested, deal primarily with familial problems, and the dramatic rites of the festivals appear to provide both a ritual acting-out of forbidden Oedipal fantasies engendered in the Brahmanical patrilineal extended family, and also a re-statement of familial morality. The festivals are arranged by *ad hoc* assemblies of interested Brahmans and attended by almost all in the street.

The Brahmans also administer the village temple dedicated to the Dravidian goddess Ūrideichiyamman. This temple is a kind of nerve-centre of the village. It is the most sacred building, situated in the middle of the village. All castes owe allegiance to the deity and participate in her festival in May. Public assemblies involving more than one caste take place in the yard of the temple, and it is there that low-caste offenders are tried and punished by the Brahmans. Unlike the Sanskrit deities, who are concerned primarily with the Brahmans' private familial morality, this deity controls the harsh forces of nature which can bring blessings or curses on all villagers irrespective of caste. She is the goddess of epidemics, and of female, animal and crop fertility. She guards the village from outsiders, protects its moral law, and is particularly concerned with the maintenance of right relations between the castes. This being so, it is perhaps significant that the funds expended on the annual festival are derived either from offenders against village law or from outsiders who have economic relations with the village. Fines, extracted in cash or kind by the Brahmans from lower-caste offenders, form the major source of the funds. Another source comes from the revenue department of the government. Some coconut trees growing beside the main road are the property of the District Board, and a revenue official annually auctions the nuts to villagers. By common consent, these are each year bought for a low price, agreed on in advance by the Brahmans. After the officer's departure, the coconuts are re-auctioned, and the profit devoted to the temple fund. A third source of funds comes from peasants of Rāmnād District, who in the summer drive ducks northward into the delta and pay a fee to graze them overnight in the fallow rice-fields of landlords. Finally, the fish in the village bathing-pools (owned jointly by the Brahmans) are annually auctioned to professional fishermen from outside the village, and the profits from this sale, too, are devoted to the temple funds.

2. *The non-Brahmans*

The Kōnāns formerly had their own caste organization. Even today, all of them are kin; they comprise five small, shallow, exogamous patrilineal groups plus a number of affinally-attached households, all linked by multiple affinal and cognatic ties. Until about the 1880's, the Kōnāns were localized in Adichēri, a street of adjoining houses built on sites owned by the Brahmans. They did not intermarry, or interdine equally, with the households of other castes.

The Kōnāns had a headman (*talaivan*), at first appointed by the Brahmans but later hereditary in one patrilineal group. A link between Brahman administrators and Kōnān servants, he was obliged to call Kōnāns for collective work such as the grazing of cattle in the summer season and to summon offenders to the village temple courtyard for individual or collective punishment by the Brahmans.

For the conduct of their private affairs, the Kōnāns had an assembly of the heads of households. Unlike the Brahmans' informal and sporadic assemblies, the Kōnāns met each new-moon night in the courtyard of the village temple and brought into open discussion current disputes regarding theft, debt, adultery, assault, slander or infringement of the religious rules prohibiting interdining or sexual relations in other castes. Emergency assemblies were also held when grave disputes occurred. The headman acted as a guide to the proceedings and pronouncer of judgements, but he could not adjudicate without the consent of the assembly at large. Small offences were punished by fines; grave ones by temporary or permanent dismissal from the village, for which the Brahmans' consent must be given. Disputants who were dissatisfied with the assembly's decision might take their case for adjudication by their own Brahman masters.

At some remote period, the village goddess was the Kōnāns' private caste deity. Even after the Brahmans took over her patronage and instituted the annual, multi-caste festival, they continued to worship her separately as well. They conducted a private festival in January and assembled in the temple for special offerings and gift exchanges after marriages and funerals.

39

The Barbers, Potters, Carpenters and Village Temple Priests formerly lived on the west side of Barbers' Street on land owned jointly by the Brahmans. Each household belonged to a caste group of related families distributed in six or eight neighbouring villages. Besides settling marital and other disputes within the caste and protecting its religious laws, each group was concerned to prevent encroachment by one family on the area of service of another and to protect the service-rights of the whole group from encroachment by other households of the caste in other areas. Through a hereditary headman, the group might negotiate with the landlords of different villages for the removal of a family from one village to another if numbers made this desirable. They might also form a committee of appeal to the landlords of a particular village if these failed to fulfil their obligations toward the specialist family in their village.

In the late Marātha and early British periods, landlords might not evict a specialist family without the consent of the specialist community. Their freedom to do this was acquired in the latter half of the nineteenth century with the development of the concept of private property in land. Unlike the Kōnāns and the Pallans, who as serfs were entirely under the administration of their landlords, the specialists appear, in the Marātha period, to have had certain rights to direct protection by officers of the government. For their shares in the village's grain harvest were distributed to them in the presence of government officers at the time of the collection of revenue. During British rule, the specialists lost any right to governmental protection which they may have had, and became, like the other castes, mere tenants who could be evicted at will. Today, with the increase in numbers in their castes, the mobility of many families, the departure of some to the towns, and the powers of eviction of landlords, the specialist caste groups have lost their functions of settling disputes and fixing areas of service. They persist merely as informal groups of kindred scattered over wide areas. In Kumbapettai, those specialist households who retain their occupations are administered directly by the Brahmans. Until very recently they have, as in the old days, submitted for Brahmanical judgement any disputes they had with the other non-Brahman castes.

Since the 1860's, individual households or small communities of many other non-Brahman castes have settled in Kumbapettai. The Kallans, who comprise one patrilineal group together with one household of affines, and live together in Akkāchāvady, at first settled their own disputes and worshipped their own caste deity in a shrine in one of their gardens. So also did the Tamil Nāyakkans, who comprise one patrilineal group together with two affinal households, concentrated in Vettāmbādi. But gradually, as families of many other non-Brahman castes became scattered about the village, some wider form of non-Brahman organization was required. With the sale of land, the Kōnāns too became scattered. Only the poorest remain in Adichēri as tenants of the Brahmans. The rest, who bought individual house-sites as these became available, are now distributed in other streets. About twenty years ago the non-Brahmans combined, irrespective of caste, to form four street organizations: Adichēri (comprising the old settlement plus the new houses by the roadside); Ambettān Street, Akkāchāvady; and Old and New Vettāmbādi. The modern organizations of these streets are no longer caste-based, but since they have taken over some of the functions of the old caste community it is relevant to mention them.

The married men of each non-Brahman street annually elect two headmen (nāttānmakkar). The change to two headmen per street is a response to demands for multi-caste representation. If only one were elected it is feared that his caste group would dominate the street's affairs. As things are the two headmen are usually of different caste. They tend to be middle-aged men, somewhat wealthier than their neighbours. Their office is no longer hereditary, and the Brahmans, who no longer hold complete economic control over non-Brahmans, have no right to depose them.

The street assemblies jointly conduct a non-Brahman festival (formerly the Kōnān's private festival) to the village goddess in January. The festival is financed from cash fines paid to their street headmen by disputants, from cesses on the sale of paddy and animals, and from a general cash levy. The eight headmen, together with interested householders, meet each new-moon night in the village temple yard and settle disputes which may be outstanding concerning debt, theft, adultery, boundaries, slander, etc. Today, no attempt is made to administer the religious laws of the castes, and unless they lead to physical violence, cases of adultery between people of different castes (which are common) go unpunished. Small disputes within the street are settled privately by street-members with their headmen as spokesmen. Major brawls between persons of the same or different streets require an immediate assemblage of all the streets.

The modern street assembly and headmen have usurped another function of the old caste community: the witnessing of marriages. Formerly, among non-Brahmans and Ādi Drāvidas, the headmen of the caste communities of both bride and groom witnessed the exchange of gifts at the final arrangement of a marriage and noted the amount of bridewealth promised by the groom's family to the bride's. [4] If, later, the amount was not forthcoming, or if after some time a divorce was effected, the headmen and household heads of both communities enforced the necessary payment or the return of the goods. Today in Kumbapettai, although each caste is still endogamous, the headmen of the multi-caste street act as witnesses in the arrangement of the marriage. Along with this change goes a further breakdown of barriers between the non-Brahman castes. With the exception of the lower-ranking Barbers,

Washermen and Koravas, Kumbapettai non-Brahmans now invite each other and interdine freely at marriages and funerals. A kind of fictional kinship has also grown up between these castes. Non-Brahman persons of different caste who are born into the village, whether male or female, call each other by the terms for patrilineal kin (who may also not be married), and women married to men of the village call members of other castes by the terms appropriate to their husbands' patrilineal kin.

The following trends are therefore perceptible in the modern non-Brahman organization. The caste community is no longer a localized, administrative or commensal unit, and has ceased to perform exclusive religious rites. These functions have been transferred to the multi-caste street (or rather, retained by the street which is now a multi-caste community). In addition, all the streets now combine for certain purposes as a wider community. Whereas, formerly, their Brahman masters formed a court of final appeal for disputants and forcibly intervened in all disputes *between* castes, disputants are now encouraged to abide by the decisions of their elected leaders and to prevent the intervention of Brahmans. These modern trends appear to be determined by the modern economic arrangements: the sale of village land to outsiders or to small peasant cultivators within the village, the rise of traders and shop-keepers, and the change from hereditary service-relationships to short-term contractual ones.

3. *The Ādi Drāvidas*

The Dēvendra Pallans form a single community divided into four streets. Although some new families have entered the village, kinship ties now link most of them. They comprise seven small, exogamous patrilineal groups distributed in forty-seven households, and thirty 'odd' households of attached affines and cognates. The Tekkatti Pallans of Long Street form an independent community comprising two small patrilineal groups distributed in eight households, and two households of affines and cognates. The two subcastes dispute for ritual precedence, have a separate social life and separate cremation grounds, and do not interdine.

Like the Kōnāns of old, each Pallan street has one headman. His post was formerly hereditary, but for the past five years the Brahmans have permitted each street to elect its own, younger headman. His appointment must, however, be ratified by the Brahmans, and they retain the right to depose him. The last headman of Kumbapettai Upper Pallan Street was deposed three years ago, after a drunken brawl in which he had been heard to ask whether anyone could tell him what use Brahmans were to the village. The headman forms a link between the Brahmans and the Pallan streets. He summons street members for collective tasks such as channel-digging, road repairs and transplanting; calls offenders for judgement before the Brahmans in the village temple yard; represents Pallan grievances to their landlords, and presides over monthly and occasional assemblies of married men of his street. The assemblies deal with marital disputes, divorce suits, and cases of adultery, assault, slander, theft and debt. They occasionally expel grave offenders from the village. Two men were dismissed during my stay, after a fight over the wife of one of them. Both were *pannaiyals* of Brahmans, who, seeing the seriousness of the case, forgave them their small cash debts and ratified the assembly's decision. [5] The headmen also witness marriages and divorces between persons of different streets or different villages. In the Dēvendra Pallan Chēri, headmen and assemblies of all the streets combine to judge disputes between members of different streets.

The Dēvendra Pallans of all four streets collectively own a shrine dedicated to the goddess Kāliamman, which stands at the head of Upper Pallan Street. The goddess, who is responsible for smallpox and female barrenness, is thought to be a younger sister of the village deity. Her festival is celebrated privately by the Pallans on the day following the end of the village festival. At the start of the village festival, a bell is rung round the bounds of the village proper to mark it off from other villages and place it in a state of ritual purity. During the seventeen days of the festival, sexual relations within this area are forbidden and no person living within it may leave it. At the end, the village is believed to be purified from sin and made safe from epidemics for another year. As a polluting caste who live at a distance from the village and must go to work in outlying fields even during the festival, the Pallans are excluded from the main area of the village, although they take part in the festival. For its duration, a religious officiant (*mūppādi*) of each Pallan street camps within the village bounds in order to be purified for the role of sacrificer which he plays during the rites. The Pallan settlement must, however, be purified after the main festival is over and its own deity invoked for blessings. Funds for the shrine are levied from fines paid by offenders and from cesses on the sale of surplus paddy to Kallan traders. As a small street of comparative newcomers the Tekkatti Pallans have no caste shrine, but propitiate the family deity of their oldest patrilineal group.

The intervention of the street assembly and its headman extends very far into Pallan life. At the slightest sign of individual nonconformity or in the smallest crisis of family life, street members bring pressure to bear and request their headman to maintain discipline. When brothers divide their property, the headman and assembly witness the distribution of every pot and pan. If a kinsman from elsewhere visits the village, he goes first to the headman's hut and only then to that of his affines. If surplus paddy is to be sold, it must be sold through the assembly and the *mūppādi* and a toll exacted from its price. Before prohibition, all the Pallans were heavy drinkers and daily exchanged a portion of their paddy gains for liquor at the Nāyakkan toddy-shop. But before drinking they assembled in a queue outside the shop, delivered their paddy to the street headmen and received back an equal number of bottles per man. Until recent years when some of the Pallans became tenant farmers and obtained slightly higher, private earnings, equality of payment and privilege for all *pannaiyals* was insisted upon. Even today, a gift to an individual Pallan must be divided equally between the members of his street.

Several factors appear to determine the lack of privacy among Pallans, their fanatical emphasis on equality, and the extreme control of the street over individual affairs. First, the equal payments traditionally made to *pannaiyals* permitted total equality of possessions and expenditures. Further, the traditionally equal roles of *pannaiyals* vis-à-vis their landlords, as dependants of comparatively wealthy superiors, produced a kind of sibling rivalry, an acute jealousy of each other's privileges. At the same time, the marked social distance placed between the Pallans and all other castes forces them to fall back on each other for companionship, so that equality of privilege and strong disciplining of nonconformists is essential to harmony.

Second, although each Pallan household is attached to a particular land-owning family, the Brahmans in many contexts deal with the Pallans as a collectivity. In particular, individual offences against the privileges of the upper castes are apt to provoke heavy fines imposed on the street as a whole, or corporal punishment administered to random individuals. There is therefore a constant watchfulness throughout the Pallan streets, especially on the part of the headmen who are responsible for collective good behaviour.

Third (in contrast to the Brahmans), familial authority and age-rank are weak among Pallans. Having no jointly owned immovable property they do not form patrilineal extended families. From about the age of seven, children contribute separately to the family income. By adolescence they are economically independent. Upon marriage, youths set up separate elementary family households and become adult members of the street, equal to their elders in privilege and responsibility. Divided as they are into numerous equal elementary families rather than into a few large patrilineal lineages within which age-rank forms the basis of authority, the Pallans require strong extra-familial controls. In external relationships these are provided by the Brahmans (whose authority in certain contexts early usurps that of the father in the elementary family). Within the street, control is exercised through the constant mutual supervision of peers.

In 1952, therefore, Kumbapettai's Ādi Drāvidas, unlike the non-Brahmans, retained separate administrative organizations for each subcaste community. But with the continual increase in the number of coolie labourers, the break-down of bonds of loyalty to landlords in stable tied-labourer relationships, and the lowering of wages which resulted from overpopulation, suggestions had already been made for a combined organization for Dēvendra and Tek-katti Pallans to demand higher wages from their employers. In other areas of Tanjore, especially on large estates in the east of the district, a number of such unions had been organized by the Communists as early as 1948. Largely as a result of Communist pressure, the Madras Government passed a bill known as the Tanjore Tenants' and Labourers' Ordinance in September 1952. The bill applied to landlords owning more than five acres in one village. It required fixity of tenure for their *kuthakai* tenants, an increase in the tenant's share from approximately one-fifth to two-fifths of the crop and, for *pannaiyals*, an increase in wages which in Kumbapettai amounted to a doubling of the existing rate. The bill was passed after I left the village, but I heard of its effects on a subsequent visit in March, 1953. Kumbapettai's landlords (some of whom owned less than five acres) at first refused to pay the stipulated sum. In any case, daily coolie labourers were unaffected by the bill. During the harvest of 1953, in response to encouragement by the local Communist member of the Madras Legislative Assembly, a labour union was formed comprising all Pallan and Parayan street assemblies of Kumbapettai and four neighbouring villages. The non-Brahman streets did not formally join the union, but non-Brahman tenants and labourers gave it their support. Under threat of a general strike, all Brahman and other local landlords were induced to pay all tenants and labourers shares only slightly less than those stipulated in the bill.

THE ENDOGAMOUS GROUP

Each caste community belongs to an endogamous group distributed in many villages. Even traditionally, the small size of the local caste community, together with incest prohibitions, must have caused at least half the population to marry outside the village. Today, with the modern separation of many households from their local communities, only twenty-five per cent (57 out of 235) of Kumbapettai's current marriages are between persons of the same natal village.

The endogamous groups of all Kumbapettai's castes were once confined to villages in the north of the modern Tanjore *tāluk* and the west portion of Pāpanāsam (see Map 2, p. 12) within about twenty miles of this village. It seems probable that the area once comprised an administrative subdivision of the kingdom. The endogamous group had no formal organization. It was merely a clearly demarcated group within which marriage, visiting (especially for family ceremonies) and free commensality took place. Its existence gave a certain unity to an area wider than the village. In particular, individual affinal and cognatic ties, cross-cutting villages, counteracted the tendency toward collective disputes between neighbouring villages. Such disputes arose fairly frequently over field-boundaries, the movement of stray cattle, or failures in hospitality to guests from a neighbouring village come to watch a festival. Disputants were supported by their villages at large, and pitched battles with sticks often resulted between non-Brahmans and Ādi Drāvidas of the opposing villages. Caste rules of non-violence prevented the Brahmans from fighting, but they bribed their tenants and labourers to fight on their behalf. Inter-village battles were however of short duration; multiple kinship obligations, which cut across village boundaries, were instrumental in bringing them to a close. So also were those specialist service-relationships which crossed village boundaries.

Within the endogamous group a certain amount of individual movement took place from one village to another. Among landlords, such movement was confined to adoption. Lineages and extended families remained stable on their sites over many generations. If a man had no son, he adopted an uninitiated boy from another family of the subcaste, of his own or another village, thus preserving the continuity of the lineage. Among the lower castes, by contrast, a serf or specialist might, with the consent of landlords, move from his natal village to that of an affine where more work was available and acquire a new attachment to a landlord there. The kinship system of the lower castes, which stresses matrilateral and affinal ties as strongly as patrilineal descent (Gough 1956: 846), and permits a high proportion of matrilocal and uxorilocal residence, reflects this kind of mobility. It contrasts with the depth of the patrilineage and the comparative weakness and narrow range of matrilateral and affinal ties among Brahmans. Among the lower castes, therefore, inter-village kinship ties provided a means of maintaining steady the supply of labourers.

With the modern mobility of households and small caste communities in search of work, and with road and rail transport, the endogamous groups of many of the castes are now distributed in much wider, divergent areas. Those of the Pallans, Washermen and Pūsālis, most of whom retain their traditional work, are still confined to their former areas. But the Kallans', Kōnāns', Nayakkans' and Fishermen's groups extend south into Pattukottai and east into Trichinopoly (up to sixty miles away), that of the Agamudaiyans to Arantāngi and Tirutturaipoondi (up to seventy miles), and scattered families of the Brahman subcaste have moved to towns as far as Bombay. In a few cases, the boundaries between regional endogamous units of the same caste-category are gradually being broken down. Thus in Kumbapettai, one Brahacharnam Brahman woman recently married a Vadama of Sirkali; one Barber has kin in Malabar; and the Smiths state that they may now marry into any household of their caste in the Tamil country north of Madura.

This social and spatial widening of the endogamous group greatly extends the mental horizons of villagers. Apart from shopping expeditions to the bazaars three and eight miles away, movement outside the village is still almost confined to visits between kin. But such visits now give some cohesion to the larger modern political units of the district, the state and (for the Brahmans) the nation, and permit the continual passage of wealth, goods and ideas from town to village.

VILLAGE ADMINISTRATION THROUGH CASTE

As administrators of the village, the Brahmans traditionally judged five types of cases: disputes between persons of the same lower caste which had failed to reach settlement by the caste community's own assembly, disputes between persons of different lower castes, offences by a lower-caste person against a person of another village, attacks by lower-caste persons upon the rights and dignity of the Brahmans themselves, and general breaches of the moral law of the village which threatened to disturb the public peace. With the partial loss of their lands and the waning of their economic control over the village, the Brahmans have lost the power to judge some cases, but examples of all of these types took place during 1952.

The most common disputes within the lower-caste community which reach the Brahmans are those between brothers concerning the division of their property, or between men one of whom has committed adultery with the other's wife. If the street assembly's decision is ineffectual, one of the disputants carries the case to his landlord, who consults the landlord of the other. If both disputants are equally at fault, the landlords effect a compromise between them and charge a small fee for the temple funds. If one is manifestly the offender, he is forced to make restitution and in addition charged a fine.

Disputes between individuals of different but similar castes are sometimes handled in the same way. During my stay, for example, a Kallan of Akkāchā-vady one night grazed his cattle in the black-gram field of his Kōnān neighbour. The Kōnān took the case to their common Brahman landlord, who harangued the Kallan, fined him, and threatened to evict him if the offence was repeated.

In recent years, if the parties to a dispute have been servants or tenants of landlords from outside the village, the offended person has sometimes had recourse to the Brahman village headman, whose jurisdiction in theory extends to all in the village. In one case, a Pūsāli teashop-keeper's wife's Kōnān lover had failed to pay him a sum of money promised in return for sexual privileges. Because of this, the Pūsāli knocked the lover on the head with a staff. Knowing that the Pūsāli would not care to admit the full story, the Kōnān charged him with assault before the village headman, who lectured both of them and fined the Pūsāli.

When a number of persons of different lower castes are involved in a dispute, all the Brahmans, led by the wealthiest and most powerful, take action in the affair. The harshness of the penalty varies with the caste-rank of the offender. Punishments are most severe in the case of offences against persons of higher caste, for these challenge the moral order of the village as a whole. An example of such a grave dispute took place fifteen years ago. A Pūsāli and a Barber one night visited the house of an Agamudaiyan widow of doubtful reputation. A Potter and two Kōnāns saw them enter and, as a joke, bribed a Pallan to beat both as they left the house, which he did. The head of the Pūsāli family (a 'specialist' who served the village and thus had no particular landlord as master) next day reported the matter to one of the oldest, wealthiest and most respected Brahmans, who assembled all the Brahmans and the disputants. The Brahman leader summoned Parayan village servants from Mānāngōrai, caused them to bind the Pallan culprit to a coconut tree, and forced him to drink a quantity of human dung mixed in water, one of the harshest punishments for offences in the Ādi Drāvida castes. All the Brahmans beat the Potter and the two Kōnāns with sticks, forced them to drink cowdung mixed in water, and fined each one hundred rupees. The Brahman leader gave two blows each to the Pūsāli and the Barber and lectured them on the loss of dignity suffered by village servants found guilty of sexual misdemeanours. In this case, the Pallan suffered the severest punishment, for he was an extremely low-caste man guilty of physical violence toward men of higher caste. The Potter and Kōnāns were of similar ritual rank to the Pūsāli and of higher rank than the Barber, but were at fault for having attacked the Pūsāli, who as a 'common man' (public servant) and a priest enjoys the special patronage of the Brahmans.

I am uncertain how murders were judged in the traditional social system. Modern practice and the theories of villagers lead me to believe that a murder committed within the village came under the Brahmans' jurisdiction, and that only murders committed by townspeople, or by landlords of one village upon those of another, reached the criminal court of the Raja. It is certain that Brahmans were exempt from the death-penalty and might suffer no fate worse than excommunication from caste. It seems probable that any murderer of a man lower in caste than himself was exempt from the death-penalty, but that other grave offences, in addition to murder, of a man against a person of higher caste were punishable by death.

At all events, the Brahmans still attempt to prevent criminal cases from passing into the hands of the police, or at worst, to mitigate the official sentence in accordance with the laws of caste. Kumbapettai's most recent murder took place in 1949. A Kōnān and an Agamudaiyan of Adichēri, who were friends, both formed the habit of visiting a Padaiyāchi wife while her husband was away from home. Both one night saw a Fisherman enter the woman's house. When he emerged, they bound him to a tree and beat him to the point of death. The Fisherman's cries were heard in Vettāmbādi, whence his father and the Nāyakkan street headman came rushing to the scene. The Kōnān and Agamudaiyan released the Fisherman and explained his offence. The Nāyak-kan street headman, unaware of the Fisherman's grave injuries, and angered that a lower-caste man of his street should be engaged in a village brawl, gave him further blows. The Fisherman then fell dead. The village headman feared to hide the case from the police, and the Kōnān, Agamudaiyan and Nāyakkan were arrested for murder. Before the trial, the Brahmans held a street meeting, collected Rs. 700 and bribed the police to release the Nāyakkan and summon him merely as a witness in the case. They then hired a Brahman lawyer to defend the Kōnān and Agamudaiyan, who were released after a verdict of accidental death.

In discussing this case, the Brahmans argued that the Fisherman deserved to die. As a man of a lower, polluting caste, he committed a serious crime in having relations with a Padaiyāchi woman. Mild jail sentences would have been in order for the Kōnān and Agamudaiyan, but the Nāyakkan (although traditionally of lower caste than the two assailants, but higher than the Fisherman) was blameless. As a headman, he had merely tried to preserve order in his street.

Most severe are the penalties inflicted upon lower-caste offenders against the traditional rights and dignity of the Brahmans themselves. In recent years, with the challenging of the caste order which results from modern economic arrangements, such offences have become more frequent. When they were able, the Brahmans imposed ever harsher penalties in an effort to main-tain their ritual rank and administrative control. Recent cases included the adultery of a Kōnān with a Brahman woman, and blows given by a Kōnān coolie to a Brahman master who failed to pay him what he considered his due. The first offence was punished by castration and death: the second, by a severe beating and the administration of cow-dung to drink. Many other cases similar to the last could be quoted.

I was for some time under the impression that whereas the Brahmans inflict heavy penalties upon lower-caste persons who offend Brahmans, and administer justice according to clearly defined if inegalitarian principles between the lower castes, the lower castes had no redress against Brahman exploitation. Gradually however I realized that, at least traditionally, this was not the case. Until recent years, the whole village acknowledged a common body of law defining the rights and obligations of the castes, which Brahmans as well as others were required to respect. Four mechanisms appear to have operated against Brahman offenders. First, some offences of Brahmans against the lower castes are regarded as breaches of their own religious law. Caste rules of pollution, for example, forbid Brahmans to enter the Pallan streets. Conversely, Pallans are themselves accorded the right to prevent a Brahman from entering their streets, for it is believed that if he did so the Brahman and all the Pallans would fall prey to disease and financial ruin. Pallans are thus accorded privacy within their streets. A correlate of this is that a Brahman's adultery with a Pallan woman traditionally merited his excommunication.

Second, when the Brahmans themselves fail to curb Brahman offenders, they may, at least in modern times, permit recourse to self-help on the part of the lower castes. Within living memory, for example, sex relations between a Brahman and a non-Brahman woman have not merited the excommunication of the Brahman. Nevertheless, a Brahman who falls foul of his mistress's friends or kinsmen cannot claim the protection of his caste, for he is disobeying a village law. Thus when two Kōnān brothers discovered a relationship between their own Brahman landlord's son and their sister they bound the Brahman to a cart-wheel, beat him, and drove both culprits outside the village. Beyond asking the Kōnāns to change their landlord, the Brahman's father and castemen took no action against them and did not encourage the offender to return until several years had passed.

Third, supernatural sanctions are believed to support the law of the village, and a subordinate who cannot obtain justice by other means may gain his ends through appeal to these. A lower-caste man who believes himself wronged by a landlord may, as a last resort, stand before the village temple and cast up sand over his head, praying 'O Goddess! my stomach is overflowing! Avenge me.' Brahmans, as much as lower-caste men, fear the goddess's vengeance in the form of disease or financial ruin, and if they know that they have broken a law they are likely to make restitution.

Fourth and most important, the Brahmans traditionally did not wish and could not afford wantonly to exploit their servants. In recalling the past, it is the mutual love between master and servant, not the Brahmans' power to make unlimited exactions, in which they take pride. Powerful economico-ritual and emotional ties bound each Brahman household to its own hereditary labourers. Everywhere in India, these relationships are likened to those between a father and his children. Sometimes, indeed, a Brahman required his servants to fight on his behalf against the retainers of another Brahman family temporarily at odds with his own. So strong were these inter-household ties, cross-cutting caste loyalties, that a landlord was often found pleading for his own servant and trying to push off the blame on to the servants of others, when a collective punishment of lower-caste persons was being meted out.

But today, ugly incidents sometimes result from the Brahmans' continuing attempt to enforce a legal system which is in part now inappropriate to modern economic arrangements. At other times, they are now unable to administer the traditional law. This is particularly the case in Akkāchāvady and Vettāmbādi, the streets where a majority of families own their own gardens and do not fear eviction. Here the pressure is strongest to settle disputes within the streets and allow none to pass to the Brahmans. Shortly before I left, a mighty quarrel arose during card-playing between a Kallan of Akkāchāvady and four Tamil Nāyakkan and Fishermen boys of Vettāmbādi. The dispute spread until all the Kallans opposed all the Fishermen and Tamil Nāyakkans, and considerable fighting occurred. A few Brahmans pressed for intervention, but the majority nervously held back, knowing that they lacked sanctions to enforce a judgement. Eventually a Telegu Nāyakkan (of different but similar rank to the disputants, and a headman of Vettāmbādi) effected a compromise in a public non-Brahman assembly. But when they heard of this the Brahmans felt that they had lost a battle for village juridical control. Soon after this incident, the season of the village temple festival drew near. After much discussion the Brahmans decided that, for the first time in memory, they could not conduct it. The Brahman community was itself divided into factions concerning succession to the village headmanship, and the lower castes, they decided, were too rebellious to take part without a major brawl. One Brahman cited the recent non-Brahman dispute as evidence that the Brahmans had lost their right to organize the village.

The festival, more than any other event, is crucial for the maintenance of the traditional moral order. For in it all the castes give dramatic expression to the ritual ranking and distance between them, yet to their mutual inter-dependence and exclusiveness as a village community. Failure to perform the festival was a significant turning-point in Kumbapettai's history—an admission of the disintegration of the caste order before modern forces of change.

THE RITUAL RANKING OF CASTES

When villagers state that one caste is 'higher' or 'lower' than another, they refer to *ritual* rank, whether or not this coincides with greater wealth or political authority. Traditionally, ritual rank was in fact almost invariably supported both by wealth and by political power. Discrepancies did, however, exist. The Brahman Kurukkal in a non-Brahman village lacked temporal power over the lower castes and might be less wealthy than the non-Brahman administrators, but ranked ritually above them. In modern times, with the introduction of caste-free occupations and a 'secular' bureaucracy, such discrepancies are common. The difference in attitudes towards ritual rank on the one hand and wealth and power on the other thus becomes striking in modern times. Ritual rank inheres in castes by virtue of birth, and has connotations of worth. A high caste is often called a 'good' caste, and a low caste a 'bad' one. Wealth and power, by contrast, can inhere in individuals, and have connotations only of magnitude. A rich or powerful man is not thereby a 'good' man but a 'big' man; a poor and powerless person not a 'bad' man but a 'small' one. While, therefore, wealth, political power and ritual value are all principles of social stratification, it is necessary to recognize that the explicit grading of castes as 'higher' and 'lower' refers solely to ritual evaluation. Our problem is to investigate the relationships between the ritual ranking of castes and the distribution of political authority and wealth.

The ranking of castes rests on the belief in ritual purity and pollution. These concepts apply not only to castes; they run throughout the philosophy of the higher Hindu castes, particularly that of the Brahmans (cf. Stevenson 1954). Ultimately, whatever its explicit rendering by a particular sect or regional group, this philosophy appears to involve a dichotomy between those objects, experiences and impulses which aid union with the divine, and those which hinder such union. In the latter category fall all aggressive and libidinal impulses, the body itself (especially when robbed of life and soul), the whole of the material world in its economic aspect, and all activities which might chain man to the material world and prevent spiritual growth leading to release (*mōksham*) from rebirth. In the former category fall the soul itself, divorced from material and sensual motives, and ritual acts and objects designed to overcome attachment to the world and the senses and to further union with the divine.

Castes receive their ritual rank chiefly on the basis of their traditional occupations. Some occupations (the most polluting) appear to have been segregated from others directly as a result of the high-caste philosophy, as a means of ensuring that the higher castes should be exempt from acts which would endanger their salvation. Segregation of the tasks of barbers, launderers of polluted clothing, guarders of cremation grounds and removers of dead cattle, for example, scarcely has economic justification in a society with as simple a technology as that of traditional India. Other occupations, whatever their origin, are automatically branded as impure in this philosophy. Fishing is impure because it requires the taking of life for a living. The tapping of palm wine is impure because alcohol excites the senses; its use, like that of meat, is prohibited by the high-caste Hindu. Oil-mongering is impure because the crushing of oil-seeds is interpreted as the taking of life. Prostitution is impure because it requires illicit sensual activity for the purpose of gaining a livelihood.

The differentiation of other occupational groups (priests, kings, soldiers, traders, landlords, tenants, serfs) is not peculiar to the Hindu system but may arise in any feudalistic society. Ritual rank, in the traditional system, here merely gave sanction to social gradations resulting from the feudalistic division of wealth and political responsibility—with the proviso that Brahmans, as codifiers of the system, ranked above all other groups. The religious rationale for these gradations was derived from the *Purusha Sūktha*, the Rigvedic hymn which ascribes the creation of priests (Brahmans) from the creator's mouth, of kings and warriors (Kshatriyas) from his arms, of traders

(Vaishyas) from his thighs and of menials (Sūdras) from his feet. As in most if not all areas of India, the Tanjore hierarchy did not conform to this theoretical 'original' division of society into four *varnas*. But the supposed original division provided a justification for the actual ranking of castes, which with few exceptions did (necessarily) support the administrative hierarchy and the stratification resulting from unequal wealth.

In Tanjore in the Marātha period, this combination of the three bases of ritual rank (the ritual segregation of polluting occupations, the administrative hierarchy and the division of wealth) produced five categories of castes whose mutual rank was unequivocal and a sixth category whose rank varied with circumstances and was often in dispute. The five fixed categories were: (1) the Brahmans; (2) the non-Brahman aristocratic castes of rulers, army officials, land-managers and village administrators (Vellālas, some castes of Naidus and some castes of Kallans); (3) the 'clean' castes of non-Brahman villagers who managed no land (tenants, cowherds, artisans, etc.); (4) castes of non-Brahman villagers with 'polluting' occupations (toddy-tappers, oil-mongers, washermen, barbers, etc.); and (5) the castes of serfs (Pallans and Parayans). The sixth category, of traders and urban craftsmen, comprised castes all of which appear to have ranked always below (2) and above (4), but which disputed for precedence with (3) and were at various periods considered above or below them. The *mutual* ranking of these urban castes undoubtedly varied with their economic strength and the political power of their guilds.

Below category (2), the administrative, economic and ritual hierarchies appear to have been practically coterminous. Above this, the hierarchy forked, with the Brahmans holding supreme ritual rank, and the king and non-Brahman aristocracy holding authority in administrative affairs. Three circumstances, however, appear to have lent administrative and economic support to the ritual rank of the Brahmans. First, although they were less wealthy than many non-Brahman aristocrats, the Brahmans possessed inalienable rights of land-management and themselves administered their own villages. Even in non-Brahman villages, the Kurukkal held independent rights to maintenance from land owned by the temple deity; he was not a tenant of the non-Brahman landlords and need submit to the jurisdiction only of his own caste assemblage. Second, the law of the kingdom was defined as religious law; the Brahmans codified it and Brahmans played a prominent role in its administration through the royal courts.[6] Finally, the Brahmans were to some extent above the general law of the kingdom. They could be tried for offences only by their own caste assemblies and were exempt from the death-penalty.

A number of special customs characterized the Brahmans, mostly connected with their belief in pollution and their ascetic philosophy. These included cremation rather than burial of the dead, widow celibacy, the prohibition of divorce, vegetarianism, the prohibition of animal sacrifice except under very special conditions in the performance of Sanskritic *yāgams*, the practice by which individual men might seek special religious merit as ascetics (*sannyasis*), and the use of Sanskrit texts in household ceremonies. For centuries before the British period, some or all of these customs were shared by castes of categories (2) and (6), and, together with occupation, formed criteria of rank *within* each category. All castes above category (5) banned the eating of beef, the cardinal prohibition of Hinduism.

The inegalities of the system were justified by a race theory and by the doctrine of rebirth (both held by Kumbapettai Brahmans today). Members of the different castes were believed born, as a result of racial heredity, with physical, intellectual and spiritual powers suited to the performance of their occupations. The duty (*dharma*) of each individual was to carry on the occupation and observe the moral laws of his caste. Failure in these respects resulted after death in rebirth of the soul (*ātmā*) in a lower caste, or even, in cases of extreme guilt, in temporary rebirth as an animal. Excellence in the fulfilment of *dharma* led to rebirth in a higher caste. The supreme object of the Brahman was to break the long cycle of rebirths and attain union with the divine soul (*paramātmā*). It seems doubtful, however, whether the lower castes even traditionally subscribed to these beliefs. They appear chiefly to have provided the higher castes with a rationale for their privileges. In modern Kumbapettai, at all events, the non-Brahmans, although they are aware of them, view the Brahmanical theories with nonchalance. The Pallans did not appear to have heard of them, and when questioned denied them with merriment.

Kumbapettai's hierarchy includes castes of categories (1), (3), (4) and (5). The categories are listed in rank-order in Table 1 (p. 18), the names of castes traditionally present being italicized. Since the Brahmans retain a certain administrative control over the village, and since wealth differences have not greatly changed, traditional ritual rules of intercourse between the major categories are still fairly strictly observed. Ritual distance is, of course, less marked between categories adjacent in the hierarchy than between those far apart. With the exception of Barbers and Midwives, no one may touch persons of a category higher than his own. Non-Brahmans may stand near to Brahmans, but Pallans may not approach them within a distance of several feet. 'Clean' non-Brahmans may enter the houses but not the kitchens of Brahmans; 'polluting' non-Brahmans, the street but not the houses. Pallans may not enter the street of Brahmans; they approach Brahman houses by the back door beyond the cowshed. Brahmans may enter the streets, houses and kitchens of 'clean' non-Brahmans, but may not, for fear of their own pollution, enter the houses of 'polluting' non-Brahmans or the streets of Pallans. Pallans may enter the streets but not the houses of non-Brahmans in general. Non-Brahmans, in turn, may enter the streets of Pallans but will not pollute themselves by entering Pallan homes.

Brahmans may in theory distribute cooked food to all below them. In fact, each Brahman household feeds its own non-Brahman tenants and servants at marriages in the yard behind its house, and distributes cooked food to be eaten at home to the non-Brahman specialist castes at major festivals. Brahmans do not, however, demean themselves by serving cooked food to Pallans. At their own marriages, the wealthier 'clean' non-Brahmans distribute the remains of food to any Pallans who care to wait for it in the yard behind the house. In the modern non-Brahman teashops, tea and coffee are served to all non-Brahmans irrespective of caste. Pallans are served with separate glasses across a counter behind the shop. In the one Brahman restaurant, vegetarian food is served to Brahmans and non-Brahmans in separate halves of the room, divided by curtains; Ādi Drāvidas are not admitted. Brahmans will not patronize the coffee-shops of non-Brahmans, but in recent years have consented to drink coffee at the marriages of 'clean' non-Brahmans in a separate booth built in front of the veranda.

Sex relations, like marriage, are theoretically prohibited between the castes. In fact, Brahmans rather frequently have relations with non-Brahman women. Relations between Brahmans and Pallan women cannot now be effectively punished, but they very seldom occur and arouse strong condemnation. Relations between 'clean' non-Brahman men and 'polluting' non-Brahman women are overlooked unless they lead to quarrels. Relations between non-Brahman men and Pallan women are punishable by the street assemblies of both. The few known relations between a man of lower and a woman of higher caste-category have met very severe reprisals in the form of beating or killing.

In some cases, ritual rank is fixed *between* certain castes of the same category. Thus, among 'polluting' non-Brahmans, Barbers and Washermen rank below all other castes, for they may be required to serve all in polluting occupations. Similarly, in category (5), Paraiyans are generally understood to rank below Pallans. For Paraiyans have especially polluting tasks at funerals (even those of the Pallans), and Paraiyans, alone of all the castes, traditionally eat beef.

With these exceptions, however, there is much dispute concerning ritual precedence between castes of the same category. Such disputes are possible because the occupations of these castes, and their relationships with the other categories, are either very similar or not comparable at all, and because between such castes no rank-fixing relationship exists. Within a given category, each caste points to customs, myths or privileges which give it ritual precedence over the others, but in no case is the claim universally accepted. Kurukkals claim to rank higher than Brahacharnam Brahmans on the grounds that they alone may enter the inner shrine of the Śiva temple. Brahacharnams retort that only they, and not Kurukkals, are permitted to perform public sacrifices (*yāgams*) to the Vēdic gods. Smiths, Cowherds, Potters and Pūsālis have long conducted similar disputes in Kumbapettai; so also have Washermen and Barbers. Disputes of this nature were traditionally never settled, for no public occasion existed in which the rank of one caste was affirmed over that of another, and the castes which were parties to such disputes refused to receive food from one another.

As new castes entered the village they tended automatically to join the same caste-category from which they originally came. In one case, however, a new occupation led to an implicit lowering of rank. The Vellāla widow who arrived in 1952 belongs properly in category (2), of non-Brahman landlords and village administrators. Lacking money and kinsfolk, she wandered to Kumbapettai and became a servant in a Brahman house, a task traditionally not acceptable to her caste. Since she was a stranger, few people knew her caste and she was assumed to have the same rank as the Agamudaiyans among whom she settled.

As the result of a change to new occupations, two other castes have recently ascended from categories (4) to (3). They are the Tamil Nāyakkans and the Nādāns, who traditionally belonged to different regional endogamous groups of toddy-tappers. During British rule, the Nāyakkans bought the licence of the local liquor shop and earned cash in the toddy trade. As their wealth increased, they bought land and changed their caste name from Nādān to Nāyakkan, a 'respectable' title traditionally confined to certain Telegu castes. The Nādāns continued to tap toddy for sale to the Nāyakkans. With the institution of prohibition in 1947, both groups lost their occupations and became cultivators. Both now deny that their castes were ever originally tappers and state that this was merely an occupation they were temporarily forced to undertake. They now claim equal rank with the 'clean' non-Brahman castes. Their claim is not publicly rejected, for they are wealthier than most of the non-Brahmans, make substantial gifts to the temple and loans to villagers, and, together with the Telegu Nāyakkans, control Vettāmbādi Street.

The Ambalakkārans (formerly Fishermen) are a caste whose 'clean' status is still debatable. During the past twenty years they have abandoned their former occupation, but it is occasionally remembered against them. Unlike the Nādāns and the Nāyakkans, they are poverty-stricken and wield no power in the village. This is undoubtedly the reason that their claim to equality is not fully accepted. Three years ago, their inferior rank was recalled by the case in which an Ambalakkāran was beaten to death for cohabiting with a 'clean' Padaiyāchi woman. Most of the village agreed that his offence had been grave. Since, however, the Ambalakkārans are accepted as equals by the Nādāns in whose street they live, no practical discrimination is now made against them.

With the modern changes in their economic relationships, the loss of their hereditary service ties to landlords, the possibility of new occupations and, in some cases, of increased wealth, most of the other non-Brahman castes have in the past fifty to eighty years tried to raise their ritual rank and general respectability by reforming their customs. All the castes of Kumbapettai except the Tekkatti Pallans now cremate their dead. All the non-Brahmans except Kūttādis, Koravas, Washermen and Barbers have for the past thirty to fifty years prohibited divorce and the remarriage of widows. Most households of these castes have during the past fifty years begun to employ a Telegu Brahman priest to conduct Vēdic rites of marriage, death and ancestral propitiation for them after the fashion of the aristocratic non-Brahman castes. No non-Brahmans in Kumbapettai are vegetarians, but most now prohibit the use of meat at marriage feasts and other public occasions.

Such adoption of Brahmanical customs occurred even traditionally in the case of particular castes who wished to insert themselves into a new hierarchy after migration or to raise their rank in an existing one after a change of occupation. Thus for centuries, groups of Kallans, Maravans and Agamudaiyans have filtered into the delta from the south-western uplands. Some, either through independent raids or through employment by the Rajas as soldiers, gained control over lands and set themselves up as village administrators. Such successful communities formed new regional endogamous groups, reformed their customs in accordance with Sanskrit tradition, and began to call themselves Vellālas, usurping the Vellāla caste-title 'Pillai'. So well-known was this practice that it gave rise to a saying, 'Kallans, Maravans and Agamudaiyans, becoming fat, turn into Vellālas'.

But the wholesale reform movements among the lower non-Brahman castes are apparently a characteristic only of the past century. They result from the breakdown of service-rights and illustrate a general unwillingness on the part of all castes to accept low rank in the modern society. The traditional pattern of mobility was for a small group to split off from the parent caste, change its occupation, reform its customs and attempt to 'pass' as an endogamous group of an existing higher caste. The modern pattern is for many endogamous groups of the same large caste over a wide area to adopt a wholly new, high-sounding name and challenge the claims to rank of the castes above them. The Smiths of Kumbapettai, for example, have until recently belonged to a movement of the Smith caste extending over Tanjore and South Arcot Districts. It was organized toward the end of the last century by an ascetic of the caste. This man travelled throughout the area encouraging the Smiths to become vegetarian, to abandon widow-marriage and to refuse food from all except Brahmans. He was maintained by donations, charged fines from offenders against the rules, and encouraged their local communities to ostracize them. The Padaiyāchis, Pallis and Vanniyans, related castes of Tanjore, South Arcot and Madura, have been affected by a similar movement known as the 'Vanni Kula Kshatriyas' ('Kshatriyas of the Fire Race'). Organized in the 1870's, this movement propagated the theory that the Padayācchis were once Kshatriyas, reduced to servitude by Vellāla invaders. Like the Smith movement, it encouraged widow-celibacy and vegetarianism in imitation of Brahmans.

During the past twenty years, however, intercaste competition for rank has waned among Kumbapettai's non-Brahmans. This is because, as a result of population pressure and the search for work, the non-Brahman community has become an increasingly heterogeneous mixture of small groups of many different castes. Although, over the district as a whole, these castes compete for land, work and prestige, all of their Kumbapettai representatives are at the same time animated by a desire to escape the economic and juridical control of the Brahmans. The multi-caste street assembly arose out of this desire. After its formation, the non-Brahmans gradually abolished most of the ritual rules which formerly divided them. Today all except Washermen, Barbers, Koravas and Kūttādis, who retain polluting occupations, dine together at street festivals, marriages and the termination of funerals. Even the Smiths, whose caste snobbery is proverbial, now say that interdining is a matter for their own consciences and have ceased to participate in the wider organization of their caste.

This decline of caste restrictions is accompanied by a new ideology. The earlier reform movements, most of which arose in the second half of the last century, evinced a new spirit of competition and challenged the existing rank order of castes. Most of them assumed, however, continued acceptance of Hindu religious beliefs and of the general principle of ritual rank. By contrast, the new coalition of non-Brahman groups in Kumbapettai was beginning to be characterized by total rejection of caste principles, particularly of the ritual supremacy of Brahmans. Those most active in promoting the modern street assemblies were influenced by the Drāvida Karakam, a South Indian anti-Brahman, anti-religious political movement founded with the aim of establishing an independent Drāvidian State. The more extreme urged abolition of all religious observances, and particularly of the employment of a Brahman priest in household ceremonies—a custom which their grandparents adopted with pride in the effort to raise their caste rank.

Among the Ādi Drāvidas similar developments were occurring. Toward the end of the last century the Dēvendra Pallans made somewhat feeble efforts to reform their customs. They began to cremate their dead and to employ a priest of a related caste to perform household rites for them in imitation of Brahmans. Bitter competition for work and caste rank existed between the Dēvendra Pallans, Tekkatti Pallans and Paraiyans of Mānāngōrai. But in recent years the Communist ideal of a common organization had begun to appeal to the Ādi Drāvidas, and was, as we have seen, effected shortly after

I left. In a second village near Negapatam, where I worked in 1953, Pallans and Paraiyans had already in 1948 amalgamated their street assemblies with those of Ādi Drāvidas in eleven neighbouring villages to form a Communist union, inspired by urban leaders, for the settlement of disputes and the prosecution of strikes. Pallans and Paraiyans had abandoned all caste restrictions except endogamy. Worship at the caste shrine had been stopped, and younger men boasted their rejection of religious beliefs. Although their immediate policy was to obtain higher wages and fixity of tenure, the Ādi Drāvidas believed that Communism would ultimately bring about an equal division of land between households of all castes and would totally abolish caste restrictions.

During my stay, social and ritual distance between the non-Brahmans and Ādi Drāvidas of Kumbapettai continued to be great. Attached as they traditionally were through different sets of service-relationships to the Brahmans, but having few economic or social ties with each other, the two categories of castes have been proverbial enemies. Non-Brahman servants have assisted Brahmans to the full in restricting the privileges of Pallans, and Pallans have until recently refused to work for non-Brahmans. During the all-India elections of January 1952, however, common economic opposition to the landlords drew members of both groups together. Although the Brahmans were said to have commanded, and bribed, their own tenants and labourers to vote for the Congress Party, many non-Brahmans and Pallans voted for the local Communist candidate, who had support from the Drāvida Karakam and was, in fact, elected. The labour disputes a year later were instigated by the newly formed Ādi Drāvida labour union. But individual non-Brahman tenants and labourers also hoisted Communist flags in their streets and refused to break the Pallans' strike.

In these widespread labour disputes new, if temporary, coalitions were also formed between landlords of many different castes. Some Vellālan, Kallan and Naidu landlords who had previously lent support to the Drāvida Karakam in opposition to the Brahmans, found themselves allied with Brahman landlords against the pressures of tenants and labourers. Even among the Brahmans ideological conflicts were apparent. In Kumbapettai, a young man of the Kurukkal family (which has lost wealth in recent years) declared himself a Socialist and sympathized with the Communist movement. In Tanjore villages in 1952, indeed, one major conflict overrode all others: that between landed and landless. It results from acute agricultural over-population, the concentration of land-ownership within a small fraction of the population, and the failure to develop industrial employment for surplus villagers. It seems logical to conclude that such economic and class conflicts, whatever their outcome, will in the future increasingly weaken the identities of castes.

NOTES

[1] Fieldwork was carried out between September 1951 and August 1952, and during brief visits in 1953, with the aid of a Treasury Studentship in Foreign Languages and Cultures.

[2] The Kōnāns were formerly called Idaiyans (fem. Idaicchi). The title 'Kōnān' ('king') has been adopted in an effort to raise the rank of the caste.

[3] On my first day in the village the Brahmans held a meeting to discuss their policy toward me. They agreed that I should be provided with a house rent-free, given all possible facilities for my work and accorded hospitality in Brahman homes, but that Brahmans should not pollute themselves by drinking coffee in my house.

[4] The house priests (*sāstrikals*) fulfil this role among Brahmans.

[5] Among Brahmans, excommunication traditionally meant that the offending family was expelled from the subcaste and might have no further contact with its members. Among the lower castes it merely involved the expulsion of offenders from the village and their resettlement in some other village among kinsfolk.

[6] K. R. Subramania Iyer 1928: 31. In the reign of Tuljāji (1763–87), however, the German missionary Schwartz was instrumental in the dismissal of Brahman judges and ministers and their replacement by non-Brahmans.

CASTE IN JAFFNA[1]

By MICHAEL BANKS

INTRODUCTION

The Jaffna peninsula is the northernmost part of Ceylon. An arid limestone-coral formation, it has little or no surface water except during the monsoon season, but there is reasonably abundant well-water. Rice is grown, irrigated only by rainfall, while there is extensive garden cultivation (including tobacco, onions, and chillies as cash crops) irrigated from wells. There are also large palmyra plantations and a smaller area of coconut palms; these of course need no irrigation. Apart from the manufacture of Jaffna cigars, a number of garages, one cement factory, and a coconut-oil mill, there is virtually no industry. Jaffna is not, however, an area out of touch with the rest of the world; it is highly literate and has a substantial export of educated manpower to the rest of Ceylon and, until very recently, to Malaya.

Historically Jaffna has connexions both to the south, with Sinhalese Buddhist Ceylon, and to the north, with Tamil Hindu India. Today language, culture and religion are predominantly Hindu, but this has not always been so; the struggle, both military and cultural, has swayed back and forth across north Ceylon for upwards of two millennia. Not surprisingly, Jaffna is in some respects an interstitial area. Since the aim of this publication is to explore variations on the theme of caste, and caste is ordinarily an institution defined by reference to the Indian sub-continent, my contribution will be one which looks northward to compare and contrast the Jaffna system with that of South India, and in particular with the caste system of Tanjore, which lies only twenty-eight miles away across the Palk Strait. This does not imply that I consider everything in Jaffna culture to have an exclusively Indian Tamil origin. Whatever may be the current of today's cultural drift towards an increasing separation of Tamil and Sinhalese culture and social organization, it is reading history backwards to suppose that a sharp cleavage has always existed.

JAFFNA'S SEVERAL SYSTEMS OF SOCIAL STRATIFICATION

To clarify what I mean by caste in the Jaffna context it is sufficient to state that Jaffna society has the following characteristics which can be considered typical for most Hindu systems.

(1) There are a number of named endogamous strata.

(2) There is a concept of pollution.

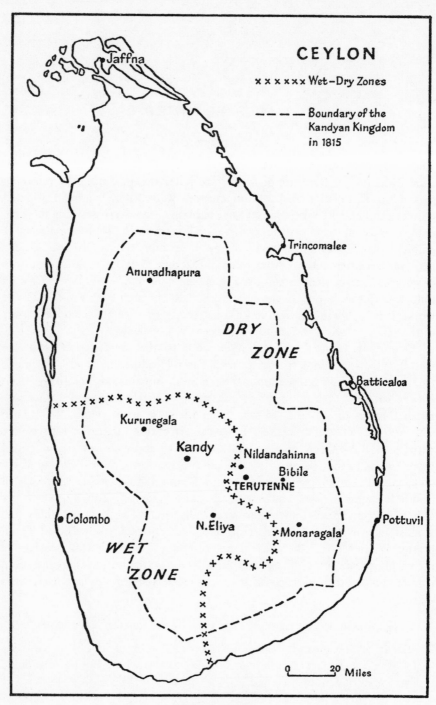

Map 4. Ceylon.

62

(3) There is a formal system of interdependence (ritual service) which links these strata together in economic, political and religious fields.

(4) The named strata are ranked and various forms of customary behaviour serve to symbolize the rank differences.

Social class in its Western sense is in Jaffna a comparatively recent growth and is still largely an urban phenomenon. In villages 'class' does not really exist, since economic and educational differentiation corresponds so very closely to differences in caste.

That it is legitimate in the circumstances of Jaffna to make this sharp distinction between caste and class is apparent from the following circumstance. The sociological concept of class always presupposes a pyramidal model—members of the 'upper' class being few and of the 'lower' class many. But a statistical model of Jaffna caste would have an hour-glass shape, the highest caste (Vellāla) being also the most numerous. [2]

The implications of this difference for social control are obvious. The largest caste has no difficulty in maintaining its position as a politically dominant group. But at the same time caste is only a limiting condition for the possession of political and economic power, and high caste is not synonymous with power as in the case of an 'upper' class.

In addition to class and caste systems, Jaffna has a third system of social stratification which operates between persons of the same named castes. This system uses the idiom of caste, but rank is dependent on acquired positions of wealth and power, though there is always a time-lag between the acquisition of these desiderata and the ascription of high rank. In this third type of stratification each caste is divided internally into unnamed, fictionally endogamous, units, each composed of a number of local residence groups scattered in different villages. These fictionally endogamous groups are viewed by the society as mutually stratified. I have termed them 'sondakara castes'; they lack not only proper names, but also a local generic name. The expression 'ennudia sondakara' means literally 'my relations'. It is commonly used to mean those who belong to 'my caste'—'caste' being here used to refer to sondakara caste, and not to named castes such as Vellālas or Pallas.

THE JAFFNA CASTE SYSTEM

In Jaffna no one village is entirely representative of the caste system. The following analysis, while based mainly on the village of Chirruppiddi, includes material from other parts of Jaffna. A single village seldom contains the whole number of castes usual for normal intercaste relations. This has the corollary that intercaste relations, and the ranking of castes, cannot be fully examined within the structure of any single village.

There are in Jaffna at least forty-eight [3] castes; no one village has more than seventeen, and eighteen villages have only one caste. Most castes are small and only occur in a few villages; only seventeen castes are found in more than eleven villages. The 'important' castes in Chirruppiddi were Brahmans (priests); Vellālas (landlords), the politically dominant caste; Kōviyars (servants of Vellālas), small renters of land and formerly chattel slaves; Barbers; Washermen; and Pallas (landless labourers), who were also formerly chattel slaves.

In this category 'important' I include not merely large castes but also those castes which, by fulfilling a specific function on behalf of other castes, come to play a significant part in intercaste relations.

Chirruppiddi contained other castes which, in this sense, are 'unimportant'. These I do not discuss in detail. Some have lost their original role in the social system—for example, the Tannakaras, elephant-keepers—others are so specialized that their intercaste contacts are confined to limited commercial relations—for example, the oil-crushers. Three relatively small castes— Pandārams (minor priests), Nadduvars (temple musicians), and Thurumbas (washermen to Pallas, Nelavas, and Paraiyars)—have been included in my discussion because of the importance of their caste occupations. In other villages these might rate as 'important' castes, so also might Goldsmiths, Blacksmiths, Carpenters, Nalavas (now landless labourers, formerly chattel slaves), Paraiyars (funeral drummers, drummers for non-Brahman temples, textile merchants, pedlars, leatherworkers, never slaves). This list does not include a number of fishing castes, some large, some small, which are not here discussed at all. In some villages the Blacksmiths and the Carpenters form a single interdining and intermarrying caste (cf. p. 17).

In most cases castes of similar name and occupation are found also in South India. Exceptions are the Koviyars, Nalavas and Thurumbas. Sinhalese castes have different names, but Tamil Vellālas are often identified with Sinhalese Goyigamas, both by Tamils and Sinhalese. Among Ceylon Tamils, Koviyars and Thurumbas are confined to Jaffna but Nalavas occur also at Puttalam (Tambiah 1954).

Castes in Jaffna, as in India, are stratified units, and the differences in rank are expressed in a number of symbolic distinctions. There are also differences of real power and wealth. It would not be profitable to make an exhaustive analysis here of those diacritic features of Jaffna caste which occur also in South India. Only those features which are more or less exclusive to the Tamils of Jaffna will be noticed.

1. *Widow remarriage*

Except among Brahmans there is a total absence of any prohibition on widow remarriage, and there is no suggestion that the woman who remains a widow is especially virtuous. Brahman custom is regarded by non-Brahmans as merely peculiar, not meritorious or desirable. In a similar way, no significance is attached to the fact that nearly all castes keep thirty-one days' death pollution. Those who know of the Varna ideology—and these are a minority—happily admit that this custom implies that they are Sudras. They do not regard this as damaging to their status, nor do they admit that those who keep fewer days (namely Brahmans, Pandārams, and Nadduvars) are on that account of higher rank, or greater purity. Furthermore no caste rank significance is attributed to the wearing or not wearing of the sacred thread. This is in fact worn only by Brahmans and some immigrant members of the artisan castes.

2. *Temple entry for Washermen*

Another abnormal feature of the system of caste ranking is the fact that temple entry is permitted to Vannars (Washermen to the Touchable castes), while Barbers (Ambattars) are excluded. This reverses the normal South Indian rule, a fact which the people of Jaffna well know. They justify the peculiarity by the rationalization that Washermen must be admitted to temples in order to decorate them with cloths. Despite this, washing is generally considered the more polluting occupation, because of the washing of menstrual cloths. In Jaffna, as in Tanjore and elsewhere in India, there is a rivalry between Washermen and Barbers, and their precise rank in relation to one another is equivocal. Each claims to be the equal or the superior of the other, while members of other castes are undecided. In these circumstances the issue as to which caste is locally favoured is arbitrary and of no special structural significance. In today's setting Jaffna Washermen are becoming one of the richest castes while Barbers remain poor; the ranking of Washermen above Barbers is thus unlikely to be reversed.

3. *An Unseeable caste*

Besides its Untouchable castes, the Pallas, Nalavas and Paraiyars, Jaffna possesses an Unseeable caste, the Thurumbas. A similar caste with the same occupation of washing for Untouchables has in the past been reported from the Tinnevelly district in Tamilnad (Hutton 1946: 199). Traditionally a Thurumba was not supposed to travel abroad by day, and had to drag a palmyra palm branch behind him at night. According to some, the purpose of this was to make a noise indicating his whereabouts; others say that he had to mark where he had walked so that his footprints could be avoided by high-caste people the next day. To an appreciable extent Thurumbas still only flit about at twilight, and many Vellālas are not even aware of their existence. Nevertheless today they do have contacts with the touchable castes. They have a formidable reputation as *seveni* men, sorcerers who kill and injure others for a fee. The only other group famous for being *seveni* men are the Muslims. Both groups are effectively outside the normal social system.

4. *The sacred–secular split in Vellāla–Kōviyar ranking*

Kōviyars and Vellālas have a curious status relationship. Although Vellālas are generally acknowledged as the superior caste, and certainly are so in secular terms, since formerly they owned the Kōviyars as chattel slaves, yet Kōviyars are recognized by all as the ritual equals of Vellālas. Vellālas will eat from Kōviyar cooking; Kōviyars may be employed as Vellālas' servants, and always cook at Vellāla weddings. Formerly Vellālas often took Kōviyar women as concubines; many of the children of such unions are today accepted as Vellālas, while others remain Kōviyars. Vellālas attend Kōviyar weddings as guests and eat there. At Vellāla funerals Kōviyars carry the bier to the burning-ground, and at Kōviyar funerals the Vellāla who has been served by the dead Kōviyar must touch the bier of the Kōviyar before the procession may start for the burying-ground. This illustrates very well the distinction between the ritual equality and the secular inferiority of Kōviyars. By touching the bier Vellālas assert or admit their ritual equality with Kōviyars; by not carrying it they assert their secular superiority.

The ritual equality is today 'explained' by an origin myth which alleges that Kōviyars are the descendants of captured Sinhalese Goigamas who were enslaved by Vellālas. Such a story implies that this contrast between the sacred and the secular rank of Kōviyars already existed at a time when the Kōviyars were slaves to the Vellālas; the only other slave castes are all Untouchables. Today, Kōviyars rank immediately after Vellālas if one places Brahmans above Vellālas, or immediately after Brahmans if Brahmans are placed below Vellālas.

5. *The ambivalent position of Brahmans*

The last suggestion may appear surprising, for in the literature on Hindu caste it is a universal assumption that Brahmans are always at the top of the caste system. Nevertheless, exceptions to this are known. Hutton (1946: 78, 79) points out that a low-caste Kuricchan of Malabar will consider his house polluted if a Brahman enters it. Again, the caste of Maha Brahmans (i.e. 'great' Brahmans) whose profession is to officiate at the cremation of corpses is regarded as a 'low' and not as a 'high' caste. In Jaffna a similar ultra-low-status group, called *kaka* (crow) Brahmans, act as priests for members of the Untouchable groups. In a similar way Paraiyars sometimes claim, both in Jaffna and in parts of South India, to possess ritual superiority over *ordinary* Brahmans. These are no doubt rather special cases though they illustrate the thesis (Radcliffe-Brown 1939) that 'purity' and 'pollution' are, in their ritual aspect, both facets of 'the sacred'.

The case for arguing that, in Jaffna, the Vellālas should rank above the Brahmans is of a different kind. Brahmans are extremely scarce in Jaffna, and with very few exceptions their professional occupation is always that of temple priest. The exceptions are mostly recent immigrants from India. To what extent this dearth of Brahmans is due to Portuguese expulsions and religious oppression in the sixteenth and seventeenth centuries is not determinable; some expulsions are known to have occurred, but the phenomenon might well be of much longer standing. More than one Jaffna man has commented to me that those who chose to emigrate to the inhospitable shores of Jaffna cannot have had much stake in the land of their origin.

The temple Brahmans of Jaffna, with very few exceptions, do not own the temple properties or temples in which they serve; rather they are the salaried servants of the Vellālas who manage the temple. The Vellāla managers serve either as a committee or in the capacity of descendants of the temple founder. Such Brahman-owned temples as exist in Jaffna are mostly in the possession of recent immigrants from India; they are located exclusively in large towns or pilgrimage centres. In villages, the usual pattern is that the Brahman-service temples are the property of the Vellālas. In some temples the Brahmans have a hereditary right to perform the pujas, but only as the servants of the Vellāla manager, whose influence extends far beyond purely secular management of the property. The Vellāla manager has a recognized right to interfere in the details of the temple ceremonial, particularly in the matter of temple festivals and their organization.

There have been a number of court cases in which Brahmans have attempted to claim ownership of a temple at which their ancestors had performed the pujas for several generations. In general such claims have been unsuccessful; the courts have held the view that ownership is vested in the descendants of the founder, usually a Vellāla. Popular opinion supports this view. In some cases the courts have admitted a hereditary right to serve a given temple.

The subordinate role of the Brahmans in their occupation has thus produced a marked dichotomy between their sacred and secular ranks (Stevenson 1954). In a sacred framework Brahmans rank higher than Vellālas on the grounds of greater purity, yet they rank decisively below Vellālas in a secular sense. This dichotomy is reflected in the behaviour adopted by members of the two castes towards one another. Vellālas, overwhelmingly dominant in numbers (over 50% of the whole population), political power and wealth, still offer towards Brahmans much of the formal deference due to a superior; for example, they give up seats and use the polite form of address. But this is only polite form.

Brahmans are not allowed to adopt superior attitudes towards Vellālas. On the contrary Vellālas have clearly-expressed views of how Brahmans should behave. A Brahman who uses the impolite form of speech to a Vellāla is much resented. Brahmans are expected to be simple, unpretentious men, mild and unassuming, given to the conscientious performance of their duties, with no aspirations to political power. They are expected not to engage in activities outside their temple work. Those Brahmans who are employed in other walks of life do not receive the respect and deference which is given to temple Brahmans. Such men are treated as if they were fellow Vellālas. The deference that a Vellāla customarily offers to a Brahman is to his office as priest rather than to his caste.

Vellālas do not hesitate to discipline Brahmans whom they consider to be behaving badly. Some of the cases in which Brahmans have claimed ownership of a temple have arisen because the Vellāla managers wished to eject the officiating Brahman in order to bring in someone new. The temple manager has a right to do this, although such rights are not normally exercised so long as the Brahman continues to give good service. Normally the existing incumbent is able to nominate his successor; usually this is his own son or, failing a son, some other near relative.

Vellālas on occasion use physical force against a Brahman of whom they disapprove. In a village close to Chirruppiddi there is a *chatram* (a species of religious charitable foundation endowed to provide assistance for travellers) managed by a Brahman, and a large secondary school which was originally established and endowed by the founder of the *chatram*. There is an annual ceremonial which links these two institutions, and an established custom that the Brahman should from time to time provide sweetmeats for the boys of the school and be generally pleasant to them. A few years ago the then incumbent was considered by the boys to be failing in these aspects of his duties. He was suspected of embezzling the funds of the joint foundation for his own purposes. A party of Vellāla boys then went and beat the Brahman until he promised to reform—a promise he subsequently fulfilled.

A further example of Vellāla control over Brahmans is provided by the fact that a Brahman will sometimes seek assistance from an influential Vellāla, such as a village headman, in finding a marriage partner for his child. To request help in this way is a form of compliment to the go-between—it acknowledges his power, influence, and subtlety. It also to some extent places the asker in a client relationship to the person asked.

As a rule, Jaffna Brahmans conform to the pattern of behaviour expected of them. When they do, Vellālas are very fond of their Brahmans and like to boast of the supposed high rank of the particular Brahmans who serve them, using this claim as evidence of their own high rank as a *sondakara* caste; it is argued that the highest Brahmans naturally serve the highest Vellālas. Because of this, relations between Brahmans and Vellālas are normally very amicable; while individual antipathies may exist, there is no trace of any general hostility towards 'Brahmans as a caste', such as is found in the Drāvida Karakam movement in Tanjore and other parts of Tamilnad. Some Jaffna Vellālas have heard of this movement, but it strikes no answering chord.

VILLAGE STRUCTURE

So far I have only described some of the more striking features by which the system of caste ranking in Jaffna differs from that found in Tanjore. Castes also differ in their internal organization: for example, Jaffna Brahmans differ from Tanjore Brahmans not only in their relations to Vellālas and in their economic and occupational roles, but also in subcaste organization. Kurukals and Ayers are not, in Jaffna, separate subcastes, but simply occupational gradings among temple priests; an Ayer can become a Kurukal after suitable training. Space forbids any general discussion of the intracaste differences, but the case of Vellālas is discussed below.

The question whether there are also more significant structural differences between Tanjore and Jaffna can best be answered by saying something of Jaffna social organization at the village level.

In Jaffna there are three distinct types of village, although the same word, *kirama*, applies to all. A 'village' in the northern part of the Jaffna peninsula is a different species of sociological entity from a 'village' in the jungle areas of Jaffna District south of Elephant Pass, even though the population of both consists of Tamil-speaking Hindus of almost identical culture. This is not merely because the economies of the two areas are quite dissimilar—villages south of Elephant Pass are dependent on tank irrigation—but also because of differences of social structure. The three main types of village in Jaffna are:

(1) Villages consisting of one ward of one caste.
(2) Villages which contain several castes but only one ward of each.
(3) Villages containing several castes and several wards of each.

The Type 1 village is found exclusively south of Elephant Pass; the Type 2 village exists in the southern half of the peninsula and also south of Elephant Pass; the Type 3 village occurs mainly in the northern half of the peninsula and in the islands off the west coast of Jaffna. From now on my discussion will centre on the Type 3 village, which is by far the most numerous and important type. The historical development of the three types and their arrangement in a logical sequence in relation to their ecology must here be neglected.

In the above classification I have used the word 'ward' in the following sense. In a typical Type 3 village, a 'ward' is a distinct residential area demarcated from other neighbouring wards by fairly precise boundaries. The inhabitants of a ward are all members of one caste. Where a village contains several wards of the same caste, these wards may or may not be adjacent to one another.

A 'village' is a territory which includes both residential and agricultural areas. The different wards of the village are scattered about in this territory and not nucleated round one centre. The households of individual wards are similarly scattered irregularly within the territory of the ward. The Jaffna ward is sociologically more or less analogous to the Tanjore 'street', but it is a much less compact residential unit.

The spatial separation of wards reflects a social separation. Members of different wards of the same village have few social relations with one another. This is especially noticeable in the case of wards of the same caste. Within any one village each ward group is jealous to preserve its social ranking vis-à-vis all other wards. Where ward groups are of the same caste, rank differentiation is a delicate matter and inter-ward social relations become minimized.

In general, despite some exceptions, ward groups of the same caste in one village do not intermarry, interdine, or have any social relations except some minor economic dealings and some degree of attendance at each other's temple festivals, [4] sometimes with the payment of part of the expenses (say a day and a night) of the annual festival. This attitude is not surprising, since such ward groups are competing for status, and the mechanics of withdrawal and aloofness, coupled with claims to higher rank, is one commonly associated with sacred aspects of the caste system.

The members of any one ward marry with and have close interaction with members of other wards of the same *sondakara* caste in nearby villages. What I have called a *sondakara* caste is thus made up of the population of a number of different villages. Conceptually each such *sondakara* caste is an endogamous closed system.

The members of each *sondakara* caste usually maintain that their own group has a higher status than any other *sondakara* caste of the same caste name.

In actual fact *sondakara* castes are not strictly endogamous closed systems. New marriages do occur between previously unrelated wards, and old alliances are cut. Apart from this, chains of marriages stretch out in many directions, so that two wards, although not themselves intermarrying, may well be unknowingly related through secondary, tertiary or more distant links. I have encountered situations in which there were two ward groups each claiming superiority to the other, even though I myself could establish that the members of the two wards were related by marriage. In theory of course any relationship of affinity implies equality in *sondakara* caste rank.

INTERCASTE RELATIONS

The Jaffna village does not have any unitary structure linking together all members of the village into one social system. The fact that ward groups of the same caste within the same village have little to do with one another means that each of the several wards of Vellālas in a village is the focus of a separate set of social relations linking Vellālas to the castes which serve them. Moreover, Vellālas do not necessarily take their servants of other castes from wards in their own village. The bonds of intercaste relationship run across village boundaries as much as within them.

For example, a ward of Vellālas may draw its Pallas from its own village, its Kōviyars from the next village, and its Barbers from a third village. The Jaffna village therefore lacks coherent unity; it is not in the least 'integrated' in Malinowski's sense of the term. Nevertheless, the village is a 'real entity' of a sort; it is more than simply a convenient administrative unit. Some Jaffna villages have recorded histories of several centuries; Chirruppiddi is traceable in documents as far back as 1645 (Foral 1920). There are also a few proverbial sayings about the characteristics of the inhabitants of particular villages. Most people think of themselves as coming from a particular village, and do not normally give the name of their ward unless pressed. Vellālas go further and normally speak as if their own particular ward constituted the whole village; the existence of other wards of Vellālas in the same village is ignored. For example, on the last day of a temple festival, when the god of the temple is pulled round the temple on a ceremonial car, I have had it carefully explained to me that everyone must help to pull the car, as this symbolizes the unity of the village. When I pointed out the complete absence of members of other Vellāla wards, this fact was brushed aside and obviously thought irrelevant. The lack of any real generic term for 'ward' probably assists this identification between the ward and the village.

A further aspect of Vellāla thinking is to suppose that the whole social system is centred and focused on the Vellālas. All other castes are thought of as satellites to the Vellālas, as their servants and retainers. Those castes which do not fit into this picture, either because they never have done so (for example the fishing castes), or because of changes in the social system (the artisan castes), are brushed aside as irrelevant. Alternatively, the more historically minded deplore the present times as a sad decline from the golden age when the Vellālas ruled all.

Traditionally, each ward of Vellālas had its own dependent wards of Brahmans, Kōviyars, artisan castes, Barbers, Washermen, Untouchable labourers, and Paraiyars. However, today, a Vellāla ward may share its Brahmans with other, unrelated, Vellāla wards; that is to say the same Brahman family may perform the pujas at two or more temples located in separate

Vellāla wards. Each Vellāla ward is still served by its traditional satellite ward of Washermen. Such a ward of Washermen will not serve, in the traditional way, more than one Vellāla ward at a time, but outside the ritualized system of intercaste obligation the same people may engage in an extensive and lucrative commercial laundry trade in the urban areas of Jaffna District. A ward of Paraiyars will normally serve a number of separate Vellāla wards, which need not be related to one another. Kōviyar and Barber wards normally serve only one ward of Vellālas or, if they do serve more than one, then all the Vellāla wards which they serve are related and recognize each other as of equal *sondakara* rank. Although the 'ritual service' links are often between individual families of Vellālas and particular families of the other caste concerned, this is really a function of the size of the groups involved, and the demand for the services provided. For example, as Washermen are fairly numerous, each Washerman family has a small Vellāla clientele. On the other hand, since there are usually very few Brahmans, one or two families of Brahmans may have to serve all the Vellālas of one whole ward. In a similar way, specific personal links are lacking between professional Paraiyars of a Paraiyar ward and the Vellālas whom they serve; this is probably because drumming is a group activity and the same small group of Paraiyars drums for all Vellālas in the ward. Kōviyars and Barbers tend to serve particular families or individuals. There are of course some members of all castes, and even some whole ward groups, which do not have these service links with Vellālas. This is particularly true of Paraiyars, a good many of whom are now specialized textile pedlars, textile merchants and contractors.

Pallas and Nalavas, although separate castes, play identical roles in the social system. They are not alternatives to each other but are found coexisting in the same village. The same Vellāla employer may employ both Palla and Nalava workmen on the same task at the same time. Formerly both groups were chattel slaves of the Vellālas, today they are free agents who work for their Vellāla masters for hire. A single Palla or Nalava individual may work for different Vellāla employers in more than one ward but it is usual to find that any one man works for only a restricted circle of Vellāla masters. Conversely each Vellāla usually employs only a small number of Pallas out of all those in the appropriate Palla ward. Pallas and Nalavas work for Vellālas on a daily wage basis and can in theory choose their own employer. But most of these people live rent-free on Vellāla land and this puts them under a compulsion to seek employment from the ward of their Vellāla landlords. In some cases Pallas and Nalavas rent garden land from Vellālas, making their payment in the form of labour. In the few cases where Pallas and Nalavas rent paddy land, it is on a share-cropping basis.

Many Pallas and Nalavas owe money to Vellālas, but this is not a symptom of bondage. Since labour is scarce, the Vellālas may have to lend the money in order to ensure labour when they want it. Vellālas also have traditional obligations to help pay for the weddings, births and other financial crises of their Untouchable labourers. This financial assistance is an obligatory gift from the Vellālas, and not, as in Tanjore (Gough 1955), a debt owed by the Untouchables to their masters. These economic links between Vellālas and their landless labourers appear to be a good deal more evenly balanced, and at the same time more tenuous, than those still current in Tanjore.

PAYMENTS FOR CASTE SERVICES

Vellālas reward the members of other castes for their caste services in a variety of ways.

Brahmans get a salary from the temple funds. In smaller temples they may also receive the offerings made to the gods. Where they assist at family ceremonies, such as weddings and death commemorations, they may be rewarded with uncooked food and sometimes with new clothes.

For their services at *rites de passage* Barbers receive payment in paddy, but these services are not confined to ritual shaving. They also include such activities as building the bier at a funeral and acting as a legal witness at weddings. In the unlikely event of a Barber being called upon for regular daily shaving he would be paid a fee in cash in addition to the annual payment in paddy.

In the same way Washermen are given paddy as reward for their ceremonial duties, and they receive an annual allotment of paddy from each household which they serve. Most Vellāla families do a good deal of their own washing; only menstrual cloths *must* be washed by the ritual Washermen. If the Washerman were called upon to wash everything he would have to be paid extra, at commercial rates in cash. A Washerman's ordinary ceremonial duties consist principally of decorating at *rites de passage*. At weddings the Washerman, like the Barber, is an essential legal witness. Both Barbers and Washermen look upon their links with Vellālas as rights rather than duties. They derive part of their own claims to high *sondakara* caste rank within their own caste from the high *sondakara* caste rank which they claim for their masters.

Kōviyars adopt the same proprietary attitude, and are normally eager to carry out their caste services at weddings and funerals (principally cooking and waiting on guests at weddings, and carrying the bier to the burning-ground at funerals), for which they are rewarded in paddy and cash. Kōviyars do not, however, receive an annual payment of paddy, and if they work otherwise as servants or labourers they are paid in cash and meals.

Paraiyars are paid for their services as funeral drummers in paddy, cash, and sometimes drink, as well as receiving an annual paddy payment for their annual recitation of Vellāla genealogy outside the house of each Vellāla family. Pallas and Nalavas have only service functions at funerals, where they build

73

the pyre and see that the body is utterly consumed. For this they are paid in cash and drink. For their day-to-day work they are paid in cash and meals.

Today, most relations with the artisan castes are strictly commercial. Goldsmiths, however, take part in a ritual prior to marriage in which the gold for the *tali* is melted, and there are rituals in housebuilding which involve carpenters. All payments made to these castes are in cash.

This present-day structure of intercaste relations is a broken-down version of that which existed prior to the abolition of slavery in 1844, and the emancipation of the artisan castes in the second half of the last century. All castes serving the Vellālas, with the exception of the Brahmans, were then divided into two groups, Adimai and Kudumai (cf. pp. 22–3). Adimai were chattel slaves, and comprised, in addition to a now extinct caste, Kōviyars, Nalavas and Pallas. The Kudumai castes consisted of Goldsmiths, Blacksmiths, Carpenters, Barbers, Washermen, and Paraiyars. These Kudumai castes were not slaves and could not be bought and sold as could Adimai. They were, however, similarly bound to serve their masters in their caste professions, and to attend the *rites de passage* of their lords' families.

The three artisan castes emancipated themselves with the assistance of the courts, which refused to acknowledge the legality of the servitudes under which they laboured. There is nothing to prevent the remaining three Kudumai castes from throwing off their services; one must therefore suppose that it is not to their economic advantage to do so. In contrast, it was profitable for the artisans to liberate themselves.

Formerly the four Adimai (slave) castes were all treated alike in some respects. For example, all had to get permission from their masters to marry (a custom still adhered to in some villages), and such permission was normally only given when both the male and female slaves belonged to the same owner; otherwise the owner of the male slave would lose the majority of the children. Owners had an over-riding right of inheritance to slave property.

But in other respects, Adimai were divided into two differently treated groups—the Untouchables (Pallas and Nalavas), and the Touchables. The Touchables were more readily emancipated, received economic aid at births, and were fed and clothed by their masters. Untouchable slaves normally had to feed and clothe themselves, getting meals and clothes only when actually working for their lords. They also had to pay their owners a yearly sum from their outside earnings.

From ancient times down to the present day by far the greater part of all cultivated land has been owned by Vellālas, but it does not appear that the inferior castes were ever legally excluded from land-ownership. The earliest surviving land registers, dating from the middle of the nineteenth century, record land holdings by various non-Vellāla individuals, including even members of the untouchable Adimai castes.

CONCLUSION

When the villages of Jaffna and Tanjore are contrasted with particular reference to caste, the most striking differences are the following:

(1) The very different roles played by Brahmans. This has already been discussed in some detail.

(2) The difference in the pattern of intercaste and intracaste relations in respect to the territorial-political unit, the village. In South India intercaste ties bind the village together, linking its members to each other by ritual and economic obligation, while intracaste ties of kinship and common-caste membership, though they establish bonds between different villages, tend to split individual villages apart (Srinivas 1952). Tanjore villages appear to be of this general type.

Jaffna villages, like Tanjore villages, are balanced systems, but balanced in a different way. It is not only intracaste ties of kinship which cut across village boundaries but intercaste political obligations also. In Jaffna, these forces cross-cut each other in such a multiplicity of directions that they cancel each other out. Every village group has kin connexions with other villages, but only with parts of those villages; and, moreover, numbers of different villages may be involved in both sorts of link. Although there are some inter-caste connexions within the village, these are again only between parts of each of the castes involved. There may even be intracaste connexions between different parts of the same village.

This total system of multiple checks and balances does not produce much in the way of village unity, but neither does it disrupt the village utterly. On the contrary it is a system of great stability. Jaffna has a reputation in the rest of Ceylon for being ultra-conservative; this despite the high level of education and the fact that many thousands of Jaffna people have lived most of their adult lives in other parts of the world. When such men and women return to Jaffna they readily fall back into the local social system. At the village level the Jaffna social system has persisted with little change over a long period, despite the most sweeping alterations at higher political levels, and the continuous impositions of European colonial rule since early in the seventeenth century.

The effect of high-level administrative and political changes upon the Jaffna caste system can be assessed by examining the fairly voluminous records left by the Portuguese and Dutch. It is evident that these colonial rulers were very cautious about altering the political basis of revenue collection which they found in being at the time of their arrival. We find that the population is categorized both for revenue and for political purposes in terms of caste; revenue collection was not directly related to the control of land. All land in Jaffna was owned outright and not feudated of the king. Taxes were levied at different rates on different castes and tax liability arose from belonging to a particular caste and not by virtue of owning land. Moreover, many caste taxes were collected by officials of the castes concerned, and these castes had pyramidal hierarchies of officials leading direct to the king. There were also territorial hierarchies of officials, but these seem to have been little concerned with the revenue. The lower castes, then, had direct links of obligation to the state, as well as local links with their masters.

Such a system is strikingly different from the much more 'feudal' type of organization which existed in both Tanjore and Sinhalese Ceylon. As a result of the administrative reforms introduced by the British during the nineteenth century the upper tier of this political structure has now disappeared; the caste groups, as such, no longer have any direct obligations to the state. But this development has left relatively unaffected the secondary, local level of the traditional structure, the village system of intercaste relations focused on the Vellālas. The Jaffna system imposes upon the individual a much greater diversity of interpersonal obligations than does the Tanjore system. In Tanjore, the individual is committed to his village or to his caste and in a situation of crisis his loyalties are not in doubt, but the Jaffna man has too many divergent and intersecting ties for any sharp polarization to occur.

It is characteristic of the factions within the wards that they are extremely unstable. Individuals constantly change sides in their manœuvres for personal position. This in turn is related to the client–patron system (which operates both within and between castes), which also is part of the multiple cross-cutting structure of personal obligations. People try to have as many patrons as possible, and in turn patrons try to have as many clients as they can. Reinsurance is the order of the day. But the more patrons a man has, the more his loyalties conflict, and the less likely he is to be a willing partner in any particular struggle. If too much pressure is put on him he is likely to desert. It is noticeable that in faction struggles it is Untouchable labourers and Kōviyars, the castes with the fewest patrons per man, who are most assiduous on their masters' behalf.

The contrast in the type of 'balance' prevailing in the social systems of Jaffna and Tanjore may be illustrated by considering their characteristic 'explosion' points. What are the situations which result in fighting and the use of violence? In Tanjore, when fights occur between villages, all members of the village, irrespective of caste, support their own village against the enemy village. On the other hand, when caste disputes occur in Tanjore a polarization of castes occurs. For example, all Brahmans unite to impose their punishment on the Pallas; and although the Brahman master of an offending Palla may plead for his servant he will not actively defend him and fight against his caste-mates. But in Jaffna fights between villages never occur, nor are there ever fights between two wards of the same caste within a single village. The violent conflicts that do occur are of two main types.

(1) There can be faction fights between two factions of the same ward—that is between members of the same caste in the same ward. In such cases members of other castes get drawn into the battle because of a client–patron relationship with some of the principals.

(2) Disputes may originate in a Vellāla rebuking a Palla or other Untouchable labourer who is not his own client. In such cases a Vellāla patron of the low-caste labourer will come to his support. The dispute may then develop into a faction fight with the two Vellālas leading rival mixed-caste factions. Obligations between patron and client normally override considerations of caste solidarity. Gross sexual offences such as that entailed in a Palla man's having sex relations with a Vellāla woman may indeed produce a complete polarization of hostilities along caste lines. But even here the antagonism does not go beyond the ward. In such a case we may find all the Vellālas in one ward attacking all the Pallas in another ward, but the neighbouring wards of the same villages will not become involved.

In short, in Jaffna, the focus of local solidarity sentiment is to be found in the residence group of the caste—that is the ward—not in the village as a whole. By contrast, in Tanjore, tension is greatest between villages and between castes of the same village. This appears to confirm the view that the effect on the Jaffna system of many cross-cutting ties is to reduce the level of tension both between villages and between castes, but that this has the effect of increasing social tension within the local residence unit.

NOTES

[1] The fieldwork on which this essay is based was financed by the Anthony Wilkin Studentship, a grant from the Royal Institute of International Affairs, a grant from Clare College, Cambridge, and a grant from the Ministry of Education under the Further Education and Training Act. The analysis of the material was financed by the William Wyse Studentship of Trinity College, Cambridge. One year was spent in Chirruppiddi village, and six months further south in the Kilinochchi colony.

[2] In India too the dominant caste is often the most numerous. Caste statistics for Sinhalese Ceylon are lacking but in Kandyan areas the Goyigama (who are the dominant caste in the same sense as are the Jaffna Vellāla) are certainly the most numerous group (see Bryce Ryan 1953).

[3] These figures and some other details are derived from a questionnaire distributed to all village headmen in the Jaffna peninsula, excluding Jaffna town. It was a total survey, not a random sample. The return was 84·5 % complete by population covered and 90·0 % complete by the number of villages covered. No other data are available, as no questions have been asked about caste in censuses subsequent to the Census of 1832.

[4] This is exclusive of such temples as celebrate their festivals on an expensive scale with many musicians and dancing-girls. Elaborate festivals of this sort attract large crowds from many miles away; some young men travel many miles night after night to see the girls and listen to the music.

THE FLEXIBILITY
OF CASTE PRINCIPLES IN A
KANDYAN COMMUNITY

By NUR YALMAN

INTRODUCTION

In Colombo one is likely to hear that 'caste' is no longer very important, and that in any case it is disappearing. Yet the concepts and strictures of 'caste' are still of central interest to the Sinhalese and—at least in the villages of the Dry Zone—they retain remarkable potency.

In this essay, I am concerned with the analysis of the two essentials of caste: first, the principle of endogamy and, second, ritual status. Both these principles—which appear to be rigid codes—are extremely flexible and adaptable. And therein lies their real strength. I describe how they remain intact even when conditions tend to contradict and undermine them. The material is presented against the background of a Kandyan Sinhalese village in the remote Walapane district of Ceylon. The name of the locality is fictional, as are all the personal names in the essay.

The Sinhalese are the most numerous of the peoples of Ceylon.* The Tamils who form the second largest group are ethnically similar but are clearly distinguished by linguistic and cultural differences. The Tamils speak a Dravidian language and are Hindu by religion; the Sinhalese speak an Indo-European language and are predominantly Buddhist by religion. The Kandyans are the Sinhalese-speaking inhabitants of the central and north-central parts of the island which formed the Kandyan kingdom at the time of its annexation by the British in 1815. The Kandyan dialect differs somewhat from the Sinhalese spoken in the 'Low Country' provinces of the south-west, and the Kandyans in general think of themselves as guardians of the pure traditions of the Sinhalese people.

1. *The village of Terutenne*

The bazaar of Nildandahinna is at the end of a motor road which winds along halfway up the side of a mountain and then leads nowhere. Above Nildanda-

---

* Census Figures 1953:

Total Sinhalese	5,621,000
Total Tamils	1,898,000
Kandyan Sinhalese	2,157,000

hinna, in the direction of Nuwara Eliya, are some tea-estates run mainly by South Indian Tamil labour. Below the bazaar, in deep precipitous valleys, are many villages. Terutenne is one of the most remote and can be approached only by three hours' arduous walking up and down the hills.

Looking down towards the village from the hills above, one notes that it is divided into various clusters and that the residential areas spread on two sides of the valley. The entire lower portion of the hills and the bottom of the valley consist of irrigated paddy fields. Indeed, the hamlets are placed around the paddy fields as if on the sides of a small lake. This is Terutenne which is spoken of as a *gama*, but at the same time each hamlet (with a separate name) is a *gama*.

There is a certain 'unity' to Terutenne as a whole (though it is internally highly diversified) and this unity is indicated in the annual after-harvest rituals to which only members of Terutenne contribute. It is quite possible to leave the village and settle in another, though normally people will not do so. They have kinship ties and property interests in Terutenne which could be prejudiced.

In 1955 Terutenne contained five named, distinct castes:

Table 2. *Castes in Terutenne*

Caste	Population	Dwellings
Goyigama (cultivators)	969	174
Baddē (Beravāyo) (tom-tom beaters)	146	27
Hēna (washermen)	30	7
Valan kārayo (potters)	38	3
Āchāri (blacksmiths)	19	3
Total	1202	214

In the next village there were also a caste of Vahumpura (jaggory-makers) and these six castes are among the most common in the Kandyan country. From the standpoint of the villagers, the Kandyan castes could be separated into three layers: the 'good' caste (Goyigama) is the highest and the majority of the population belong to it. Next come the 'low castes' which are polluting, but 'better' than the very lowest grade. These are the 'working castes' mentioned above, and others could be included (Ryan 1953: 94, Nos. 9–18). The lowest grade was not represented in Terutenne; it includes the Ahikuntakayā (itinerant snake-charmers), the Kinnarayā (mat-weavers) and the Rodiyā (itinerant beggars) (Ryan 1953; Raghavan 1951, 1953).

The village as a whole is governed through a village headman, a man of Goyigama caste, who is appointed by the Government agent of the Nuwara Eliya District on the recommendation of the local Divisional Revenue Officer (D.R.O.). The village committee also has certain political power and functions. This is an elected body somewhat analogous to an English rural district council. A single committee has jurisdiction over a number of villages; its primary duties are concerned with welfare schemes. Village committee members are persons of considerable influence. All the Terutenne members were of Goyigama caste, though a man of Washerman caste contested one of the seats and received some Goyigama support.

Minor disputes can be dealt with locally by the village headman, who is authorized to impose small fines. More serious affairs are taken to the rural court, which is not subject to control by village officials.

2. *Religion*

Most Kandyan Sinhalese are Buddhist by religion. In important respects, however, Kandyan Buddhism and Tamil Hinduism are closely related even though the two creeds are formally opposed to one another. Many of the Sinhalese castes—the Washermen, the Tom-tom Beaters, etc.—have their Hindu counterparts, and the religion of the 'Buddhist' Sinhalese includes elaborate rituals addressed to 'Hindu' deities. A Buddhist temple is known as a *vihāra* and has a Buddhist priest (*Bhikku*) as incumbent. But Sinhalese communities also contain 'Hindu' temples known as *dēvāle* (or *kōvil*) which have a *kapurāla* as incumbent. The *vihāra* always contains an image or images of the Buddha, but these may be flanked by images of various gods and goddesses (*dēvā*, *dēvi*) who are said to be the Buddha's assistants. These deities have their equivalents in the Indian pantheon. Thus the Sinhalese Kataragama is the Tamil Subramanya, Pattini is the Hindu Kāli, and Hindu Viṣṇu is even recognized under his own name (Cartman 1957, ch. v).

Such deities are subordinate figures in the *vihāra* but they are the principal deities of the *dēvāle*. In urban centres the *dēvāle* deities are likely to be 'major' gods and goddesses such as the above. In contrast, in village temples one finds purely local deities. Sometimes one meets a figure with no name at all other than that of *gama dēvayā* (village deity). Yet such local gods too may be said to be 'just the same' as one or other of the well-known 'Hindu' deities.

The two systems, *vihāra* and *dēvāle*, are essentially separate. The villagers say that the Buddha is concerned with the next world and that it is useless to ask him for benefits in this life. But the *dēvāle* is concerned with this present existence. The *dēvāle* deities must be worshipped so as to prevent immediate disaster and to bring benefits here and now.

There are no Brahmans among the Sinhalese, and the priesthood is not confined to a single caste. A Buddhist priest is a member of a strictly celibate monastic order. Some orders are open to all castes. The initiate formally renounces his former kinship ties and receives a new Pāli name.[1]

A *dēvāle* priest (*kapurāla*) is not a member of a religious order but rather a professional religious specialist. A *kapurāla* may marry and, in becoming a priest, he does not renounce his caste membership or his kinship affiliations.

In Terutenne the *kapurāla* were always members of the highest caste, the Goyigama.

In 1955, Terutenne had two *vihāra* and one *dēvāle*. The Wekumbura *vihāra* was owned by the Amarapura Nikāya order of priests, and had an incumbent of that order. The Maluvēgoda *vihāra*, in another section of the village, belonged to the Siam Nikāya order. These different orders correspond to sectarian cleavages in the Buddhist priesthood but the laity is not so divided. Individuals ordinarily worship at the nearest temple without regard to sect. Each *vihāra* is controlled in its secular affairs by a group of lay benefactors (*dāyākuyo*) who elect special Temple Society officers for this purpose.

3. *The abolition of service tenures*

Lists and descriptions of the various Sinhalese castes are given in Ryan (1953). My concern is to show the interrelations of such a system of castes within a single community. Before proceeding to this main theme I must give something of the historical background.

Down to 1815 Terutenne lay within the dominions of the Kandyan kingdom. The organization of this kingdom has recently been described by Pieris (1956). Caste was there closely related to the tenure of land. All paddy land was held on some form of service tenure (*rājakāriya*). Sub-enfeoffment was possible and the great barons of the realm, who in theory held their estates from the king, had tenants and sub-tenants of their own.

The various tenants performed their respective caste duties as part of the obligations incurred through tenancy. The relative status of different castes was made explicit in the order of precedence prevailing in various officially sanctioned annual ceremonies. At times the king might lower the caste rank of an entire community (Ryan 1953: 217). One reason why caste status is today a matter for dispute is that the central government no longer lays down caste precedence.

The celebrated Kandy *perahära* is an example of a precedence ceremonial which has survived to the present day (*R.K.P.C.* 1951: 108), but the various caste groups are today paid for their services and the low castes tend to complain of their 'degrading' ceremonial duties.

The traditional system of service tenures which rendered caste service obligatory was gradually abolished as a result of various British nineteenth-century enactments. There still remain however a few temple estates, *vihāragam* and *dēvālagam*, where the former general pattern may still be recognized (Hocart 1931; Ryan 1953: 211 f.; Pieris 1956: 74).

But though the feudal organization has disappeared and caste service is no longer obligatory, the castes are still perpetuated as distinct, almost endogamous, named groups, each having a particular ritual status. We must therefore consider what elements give the system its strength and resilience.

4. The caste communities

While Terutenne is larger than most Ceylon dry-zone communities the caste composition is not unusual. The dominant caste is, as in most localities, the Goyigama. All castes engage in paddy cultivation, but the low castes, being specialists in certain occupations, have an additional source of income.

Those among the low castes who still pursue their traditional calling undoubtedly do so for economic reasons, but we cannot isolate economics as the sole factor in the perpetuation of caste.

In Terutenne, in 1955, none of the low castes held their lands on service tenure, but there is definite evidence that all these castes (except the Potters) were already present in the village in the middle of the nineteenth century. The Potters are known to be more recent arrivals. Each of the low castes formed a distinct sub-community.

The Tom-tom Beaters lived in a named hamlet (Baddegama) which was separated from the main village of Terutenne by a stream not unlike a moat. The Washermen, too, lived in a distinct cluster some way removed from the Goyigama. The Potters lived mainly in one enormous compound in the midst of Goyigama households. The Blacksmiths (who, incidentally, were very rich) inhabited some houses on the edge of the village.

I shall consider each of these groups in turn with regard to the following criteria: (a) general nature of the community, (b) service duties, (c) caste distinctions, (d) breaches of caste endogamy.

The Washermen (Hēna)

(a) Members of this community lived together in one cluster of houses and were all closely interrelated by descent and marriage. All the Washermen, with one exception, pursued their traditional calling. The exception was a very wealthy old man who had no need of the extra income.

(b) The service duties of the Washermen may be divided into public and private services, as shown in the Table opposite.

(c) The Washermen of Terutenne were a single kin group. Their distinction from other communities around them was expressed (i) in a tradition which related how they came to be Washermen, (ii) in their caste occupation, which carried well-understood connotations, and (iii) in their personal names.

This last aspect is the most obvious index of social separation. The Washermen had personal names like Sudu Hēnaya (white washerman), Kiri Hēnaya (milk washerman); in contrast the Goyigama had 'princely' (bandāra) names, e.g. Kalu Banda (black Banda), Sudu Banda (white Banda), etc. The Washermen were not all of the same economic standing. One man was very wealthy by Terutenne standards (much wealthier than the ordinary run of Goyigama) and another (called James) also possessed extensive lands and

Hēna services

	Public	Private
Occasion	1. Annual festivals at the *Dēvāle*: *An-Keliya* and *Gam Maduva* 2. *Vihāra* ceremonies: Annual: *Katina Pinkama* (offering of new saffron robe to the priest) Birthday of the Buddha Others: *Bana* (preaching) *Pirit* (chanting)	1. All *rites de passage*: birth, female puberty, marriage, death 2. General laundry
Duty	On all these occasions, Hēna provide 'clean' (ritually pure) cloths to decorate the temples, to protect the Buddhist priests from the public gaze while eating. They make effigies of goddesses from starched white sheets for *Gam Maduva*	The nature of the service is to change 'polluted' clothes into 'pure' ones They wash polluted persons as well
Reward	Payments by the Temple Society	Payments from Rs. 2 upwards depending on the status and wealth of the patron

enjoyed considerable *personal* respect. Here personal status is distinct from caste status. James, although a Washerman, was considered a religious man and was therefore elected President of the Temple Society of the *Siam Nikāya Vihāra* by a body of Goyigama electors.

(*d*) I learned of three recent breaches of caste endogamy among the Hēna. All were referred to as serious (but slightly ridiculous) scandals.

(i) A Hēna girl, who had gone to school outside the village, had been married by a public Marriage Registrar to a Goyigama man. The man was not of Terutenne and the couple did not return to the village.

(ii) This girl's brother, who also went to school outside Terutenne, had done the same. He, too, had not returned.

(iii) A Hēna girl had eloped and set up house in Terutenne with a Tom-tom Beater. The couple were ostracized by both the Washermen and the Tom-tom Beaters. Strong action was threatened but not taken. This is the only case in the village in which the 'husband' and 'wife' in one domestic household were of different caste and also both local natives.

The Tom-tom Beaters (*Beravāyo, or Baddē (more polite)*)

(*a*) This is the largest low-caste community in Terutenne. They have their ancestral paddy lands in the middle of their own hamlet, Baddegama, where most of them reside.

There are a few households which have moved out to the opposite side of the valley. These live near the Washermen and drum in the Maluvēgoda temple. A few others are near another hamlet. Outside Terutenne, there is a large community of this caste on the road to Nildandahinna. Most Tom-tom Beaters know how to drum but a dozen professional experts would have sufficed for all the needs of the village and the temples. Those who become professionals do so for the economic reward. Skills are mostly taught by the fathers or mother's brothers to the younger generation.

(b)   *Beravāyo services*

	Public	Private
Occasion	Same occasions as Washermen	Illnesses, ritual healing and exorcism
Duty	A few members of the community provide the ceremonial drumming during rituals. Also, all public announcements are made by drummers	They act as dancers, exorcists, astrologers
Reward	Payment by Temple Society	Payment, depending on status and wealth, from Rs. 5 per night per tom-tom beater upwards

(c) As with other castes the Tom-tom Beater community is distinguished from others (i) by caste name—Beravāyo, Baddē, (ii) by caste occupation, (iii) by personal names, e.g. Ukkupina, Rangi, Ranbandiya. Furthermore, in Terutenne, the Tom-tom Beaters lived in a specific hamlet named after their caste Baddegama. All who live in Baddegama are *ipso facto* Tom-tom Beaters unless proved to be otherwise.

Only 14 individuals out of a total population of 146 owned paddy land in 1955. These owned 3·15 *pāla*[2] in aggregate. The richest member of the community was mistress to the village headman and had received gifts of land from him.

Recently there has been a move towards greater caste solidarity and a communal organization called the 'Tom-tom Beaters' Welfare Society' has come into being. It has elected officials on the model of the Temple Societies, ut its real intention has little to do with caste regulation. The idea is to obtain monetary support from the Government Rural Development Department.

(d) A case of an ostracized Tom-tom Beater living openly with a Hēna woman as 'wife' has been mentioned above. There were also some Tom-tom Beater women who were regularly visited by Goyigama men and such relationships may become semi-permanent. In these cases, however, the women are not regarded as 'wives'; the men ostentatiously pretend not to eat with the women.

Blacksmiths (*Āchāri or Kamal-kārayo*)

(a) and (c) This group is the smallest of the low castes and also the richest. It is distinguished by caste name, caste occupation, and personal names.

POLYTECHNIC OF WALES LIBRARY THE TREFOREST

It consists of a single extended family making up three households. Hingappu, now one of the wealthiest men in the whole of Terutenne, came originally from another village and married uxorilocally. On the death of his first wife, it was his mother-in-law who sought out another woman for him. His present household consists of himself, his second wife and his original mother-in-law. Such domestic arrangements are quite characteristic of Terutenne among all castes. Hingappu owns 20 *pāla* of land, much of which is let out to share-cropping tenants among whom are some poverty-stricken high-caste Goyigama.

Subtle problems of etiquette arise here. The high-caste Goyigama labourers treat their Blacksmith landlord as if he were of higher caste than themselves. In his presence, they make place for him and allow him to sit while they stand. This is the reverse of traditional custom. On the other hand, in a public place these same Goyigama labourers would be embarrassed to be quite so deferential to Hingappu. In such circumstances, though they would not give up their places specifically to Hingappu, they would at least get up and stand themselves.

(b)   *Āchāri services*

Occasion	Public	Private
Occasion	Same occasions as other castes	Manufacture of utilitarian objects: ploughs, knives, axes
Duty	Cleaning the weapons of the saints; making new metal bowls for priests	
Reward	No payment: free offerings by the blacksmiths	Individually ordered and paid for

(d) There are no cross-caste sexual unions among Terutenne Blacksmiths.

Potters (*Valan-kārayo*)

(a) and (c) This community, like the Blacksmiths and Washermen, consists of a group of very highly interrelated kinsmen (Fig. 1). They claim to have arrived in Terutenne forty years ago. There were then no other potters for miles around. It was Punchihatani, the old woman, who first settled with her daughters and sons-in-law after the death of her husband. Having found a good location for their trade their descendants have also remained in Terutenne. They own no paddy land, but merely the garden and house in which they live. Most of them live in the same compound. All the Potters work paddy land but only as labourers or share-croppers. All also engage in shifting cultivation. The caste activity, pot-making, is very remunerative and the wares are sold for money. The prices of the larger water pots go up to Rs. 2.50. The smaller cooking pots are cheaper and may be sold for 75 cents.

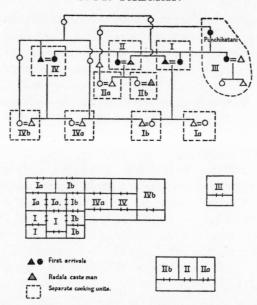

Fig. 1. The Potters of Terutenne. The Potter community comprises ten separate cooking units grouped in three households. The lower part of the diagram shows the arrangement of the rooms in these three buildings and the ownership of the rooms.

The upper part of the diagram shows the kinship connexions between the room owners. The six individuals who are not shown as belonging to any cooking unit are not resident in Terutenne.

(b)   *Valan-kārayo services*

	Public	Private
Occasion	Same occasions as other castes	Sale of pots
Duty	Making new pots for priests and for the rituals in *dēvāle*	
Reward	No payment: free offerings	Prices noted above

(d) As may be gathered from the kinship chart, most recent marriages have been between very close kinsmen. But in one case, an outsider from the Kandy district, who claims to be of the highest grade of the high caste (Radala: the rank of feudal lords), has settled uxorilocally in a Potter household. Because he is an outsider, the village is unconcerned as to what happens to him. Etiquette raises problems. He is usually identified with the Potters and treated as such. At other times he gets the treatment of any other 'poor' Goyigama.

So much for the low castes. In Terutenne these are all relatively small, highly interrelated, distinct communities. Their *esprit de corps* is expressed in their traditional calling, in their names and in their associated mythology. I do not consider that their economic function can be held to explain their survival, for many low-caste individuals do not continue the caste occupation. Nor can it be said that the low castes are essential for the ritual life of the community. High-caste people often wash their own clothes and some temples can do without Tom-tom Beaters. [3] It would be more accurate to claim that the public and private services of low-caste groups are utilized because they happen to be in the vicinity. Let me now turn to the high caste.

The Cultivators (Goyigama)

The Goyigama are the most numerous caste in Terutenne. They are extremely diversified in wealth, land-holding and occupation: there are some wealthy landlords but also many landless persons; there are school teachers and boutique-keepers. Apart from the distinctive caste name and the jealously preserved modes of speech and behaviour vis-à-vis the other castes, there are few observable symptoms of group solidarity among the Terutenne Goyigama.

This caste community is itself highly stratified (cf. Ryan 1953: 93–103). In Terutenne three wide grades—without distinctive names—are recognized. The 'highest' are a few aristocratic families; these are followed by ordinary 'good' people—this is the largest grade; the 'lowest' are those associated with serfdom. These distinctions are similar to the separation of the castes. The aristocrats do not only have prestige, but are 'pure' (pirisithu) and 'good' (honda); the lowest grade is 'impure' (apirisithu) and 'bad' (naraka) in a metaphysical sense.

'Caste' is not merely an appellation whereby one may refer to groups of people. It is a quality. One is not merely a 'member' of the high caste, but is 'high-casted'. The quality resides in the blood. And blood is graded from very pure to extremely polluting. It is not merely the 'low castes' who have naraka or apirisithu blood, but also some high-caste persons may be worse than others. Hence, although the three grades of the Goyigama are not separate endogamous groups—in Terutenne—the principle of gradation is based on caste ideas. Ordinary people will speak of these grades among the Goyigama as jāti (caste), but the more precise usage would be vangsa (pedigree, ritual status). The aristocrats are the vangsa adipati (pedigree lords); the 'low' are the vangsa näti minissu (lit. people without pedigree).

As a justification for the internal hierarchy within the Goyigama, people appeal to the past—the time of the Sinhalese kings (Sinhala Rājaruvo Kāli). It is beliefs about the past which provide the blueprint for the present. The aristocrats are of high rank because they are descended from families which owned much land and were feudal lords. They had many serfs. Some of the aristocrats provided the provincial governors of the Walapane Division (Mohottāla) and there were others who were wealthy and closely related to them. The descendants of these families have carefully preserved their titles.

Such titles are variously referred to as *pelapata, paramparā nāma, vasagama* or *mudiansē nāma.* [4]

While the would-be aristocrats of 1955 thus claimed that their *vangsa* was inherent in their ancient heritage, they would also claim that the 'low' Goyigama were of lesser *vangsa* because their forefathers had been serfs. These serfs were no longer bound by feudal (*rajakāriya*) laws but 'respectable' people would not intermarry or interdine with them. And their 'lowness' was evident in their names, for they were distinguished from other Goyigama —so it was claimed—by their lack of ancient titles and *vasagama* names. They had been the 'working people' (*väda kārayo*) like the low castes.

Such claims are in the nature of myths. There is undoubtedly plenty of evidence—from documents on Kandyan history, the constitution of the kingdom, and grain tithe registers kept during the nineteenth century— to prove that the claims of this kind might be historically justified (Pieris 1956: 171 ff.), but what is significant is that such claims should still be pressed even though the Kandyan kingdom and its organization is past history. How are these titles inherited? Are the people who claim high rank really the descendants of past aristocrats? What prevents the changing of names? These queries, which suggest the dynamic aspect of such status gradations, are considered below. Here let me merely note that the so-called 'serfs', who lacked *vasagama* names, tended to inhabit hamlets of 'low' status, in particular the Terutenne hamlet of Gālpitiya.

Now these Gālpitiya Goyigama were not only reckoned to be 'low' in status, they were also exceedingly poor. Nearly all of them worked as labourers on the fields of others. In contrast, we may note that there were some other 'low' Goyigama who had grown rich and thereupon changed their place of residence and successfully assumed aristocratic titles. And again there were some 'high' Goyigama who had grown poor. These latter were accorded little respect even though they made great show with their titles and ancient honours.

In Terutenne there were no recognized marital unions between Goyigama and members of lower castes. On the other hand, there were various individuals of doubtful and shadowy caste origin who had arrived in the village as outsiders and married with Goyigama spouses from the Terutenne community. Many of these outsiders were alleged to be of the Fisher caste (Karāva) from the Maritime Provinces but subsequent to their domicile in Terutenne they had become fully absorbed into the Goyigama community. The absorption of alien 'individuals' presents few difficulties either in Terutenne or New York. It is only when the new arrivals form whole 'communities'—as do the Potters of Terutenne or the Puerto Ricans in New York— that social barriers make their appearance.

ENDOGAMY

1. *The implications of kinship*

In this section I am concerned with the flexibility of caste barriers. The general literature on caste might lead us to suppose that such 'barriers' are like rigid fences which can be broken down by successive intercaste marriages. In my opinion, on the contrary, these caste barriers are extremely resilient. The caste rule will survive an almost unlimited amount of formal breach.

What is the nature of these endogamous barriers? How do the Sinhalese castes remain separate? There are at the moment in most Sinhalese areas no caste *panchayats* such as are found in India. Delicts concerning caste offences cannot be dealt with in a formal fashion, either in the village or in the law-courts outside. The decisions to observe caste rules in the arrangement of marriages are made by individual kin groups. Where, as sometimes happens, a family decides on a union in which the caste position of the other party is dubious, or where a family fails to excommunicate one of its members who has entered into a cross-caste union, the decision would be considered a private matter. The rest of the village would not—in ordinary circumstances —be moved to active protest. Therefore, as Ryan observes (1953: 28–9, 314), the mainsprings of caste are to be sought in the family. For it is the individual decisions of separate families which perpetuate the 'barriers'—hence the reasons for endogamy must be looked for in the nature of Kandyan kinship.

There are variations in Kandyan kinship. The pattern of inheritance, the pattern of marriage, the closeness of kin-group endogamy and the position of women all vary as between the different economic classes and as between different castes. But among all groups, rich and poor, high caste and low, kinship is recognized in all lines through all links. The sister's husband's brother may be just as important a relative as the father's brother.

Among all classes, women as well as men have claims on property. Unmarried daughters share the inheritance equally with their brothers. Married daughters may either receive their shares at the decease of their parent or be given dowries the sizes of which depend on the status of the groom. A system in which men and women have claims on all property appears to be consistent with a state of affairs in which affinal relations are greatly emphasized and kinship traced equally through both sexes.

A marriage which is endogamous to the village may be either virilocal or uxorilocal or, alternatively, the couple may build a separate house for themselves.

Each married woman cooks by herself on a separate hearth. Formal wedding ceremonies are often dispensed with but in such cases the fact that the woman establishes a new separate cooking place is itself tantamount to marriage. The kinship nucleus which forms around the woman's cooking hearth—that is to say the woman herself, her children, and her husband (or husbands) was in Terutenne referred to as a *Gē*. [6] In essence this *Gē* is the basic elementary family, though other relatives may now and again find hospitality within the *Gē*. There were 231 Goyigama *Gē* in Terutenne. Table 3 shows how they were grouped by dwelling units.

Table 3. *Incidence of dwellings containing several* Gē (*Goyigama*)

Number of *Gē* contained within one dwelling	1	2	3	4	5	6	Total
Cases	135	27	6	2	2	1	173
Total number of *Gē*	135	54	18	8	10	6	231

The kinship relations between the various *Gē* which shared a common dwelling-house varied. In only 48 cases was a married child sharing a common dwelling with a parent. Of these, 31 were cases of virilocal residence and 17 uxorilocal. Evidently the general preference was for residence apart from either set of parents.

Apart from choice as to the locality of residence after marriage, Kandyan custom traditionally permits both polyandry and polygyny, though polygamous unions are not legally recognized by the State. Polyandrous and polygynous unions both existed in Terutenne in 1955 but both were rare. (For a different finding see Prince Peter 1955, but cf. Leach 1955.)

2. *Endogamy within the kin group*

Regarded as a residential unit with a separate food supply the *Gē* is, in important respects, an independent economic entity, but the importance of kinship ties outside the *Gē* should not be underestimated. In theory, all kinsmen of common descent are expected to co-operate on all occasions, but since, in a situation where kinship is traced in all lines, the principle of common descent is likely to embrace the entire caste community, effective kinship ties are much more restricted. In such circumstances marriage plays a special role, since it is utilized to renew bonds of descent which have grown weak and distant. A marriage serves to bring back distant relatives into the circle of close kinsmen.

Kinsmen by marriage are expected to co-operate just as closely as kinsmen by descent. Marriage creates an alliance between men, and this aspect of marriage—the bonds established between male affines as opposed to those between husband and wife—needs to be emphasized (cf. Dumont 1957 (*b*)).

In Sinhalese kinship terminology the term *māmā* includes not only mother's brother and father's sister's husband but also father-in-law. The reciprocal term *bānā* includes not only the nephew but also the son-in-law. The relationship *māmā/bānā* is always of cardinal importance, but people will say that whereas before marriage it is the mother's brother who matters, after marriage it is the other *māmā*, the father-in-law, who assumes dominating significance.

In planning a marriage the father-in-law sets out to obtain as excellent a son-in-law as money can buy or influence acquire, and at the same time the son-in-law seeks as his ideal father-in-law a man of wealth who is also respectable in ritual status.

The working out of these, at times contradictory, objectives may be seen in the circumstances governing marriage payments. Normally the Sinhalese do not pay brideprice in any form. On the other hand, women are potential heirs to property. In cases where property in land is inherited by a daughter the actual management of the estate is carried on by the son-in-law. However, among certain of the richer elements in the community a different system prevails. Landlords who grow crops for sale, school teachers, village headmen, clerks in administrative offices, boutique-keepers are all people who receive their income in the form of ready cash. Among this class of people the dowry system is common. A daughter is excluded from rights of inheritance but instead she receives, at the time of marriage, a cash dowry. Management, as distinct from ownership, of the dowry devolves upon the son-in-law. The amount of the dowry varies with the standing of the son-in-law.

These dowries are substantial. A clerk may receive Rs. 500–1000, a village headman Rs. 2000. The value rises steeply as one moves into the higher branches of Government service. A D.R.O. may receive as much as Rs. 20,000. The scale of the contributions alone is sufficient indication that the father-in-law expects close co-operation from his son-in-law. In such circles property and the marriage alliance are closely bound together; everyone realizes that a 'good' alliance is possible only with a generous dowry.

This notion of marriage as an alliance has an important bearing on the constitution of wider kinship groups. It creates a tendency towards endogamy within the 'family': and this phenomenon must be clearly analysed.

The Kandyan Sinhalese use the term *pavula* for 'family'. It has various shades of meaning: it may mean 'kindred' in the widest sense—the group of kinsmen somehow related who regard themselves as 'one people' (*eka minissu*); it may mean a sibling group, together with its affines and offspring; it may mean a single married couple, with their children and grandchildren, or it may mean only a woman and her children, or even simply 'wife'. [7]

In its widest extension the *pavula* ('kindred') is only a loose association but it is not simply a vague amorphous group of kinsmen with whom one individual happens to be able to trace connexions.

Pavula members own no property in common, nor do they share a common name, nor has the *pavula* any definite structure of authority; yet the *pavula* is a group which acts (or is expected to act) in unison in all village disputes and in all those frequent skirmishes which peasants have with Government authorities. There exists a genuine sense of unity and cohesion within the *pavula* group. This is partly the result of the intermingling of ties by descent and marriage, and partly—since marriage presupposes the existence of close co-operation—the outcome of common interests in diverse spheres of communal life: paddy fields, shifting cultivation, common residence, etc.

Outsiders, too, recognize these bilateral, loosely organized, kinship conglomerations and refer to them as 'one people' (*eka minissu*) or 'one family' (*eka pavula*). They are also considered to have 'one blood'. This implies, in accordance with caste ideology, that all members of one *pavula* are of the same ritual status.

For many individuals in Terutenne *pavula* allegiance was a matter of doubt, but every occasion of dispute or feud tended to crystallize out the various *pavula* into separate observable units. *Pavula* boundaries also became apparent on ceremonial occasions. All *rites de passage*—birth, girl's puberty, marriage, death—are occasions for ceremonial feasting. Auspicious feasts are *magul gedera* ('festivity house'); death, being inauspicious, is *ava magul gedera* ('non-festivity house').

In these festivities cooking and eating are ritualized activities. As in most cultures, commensality expresses social unity. Only 'equals' and 'familiars' may interdine. It is rude for a stranger to watch a man in the act of eating. On the other hand, those occasions when members of the *pavula* publicly unite together for a feast are charged with symbolic implication. The *pavula* are here seen to be 'one people' of united blood and common ritual status. It is noticeable that at all *magul gedera* the common feast forms the central feature of the ceremonial.

We see then that there are two aspects to the unity of the *pavula*. On the one hand it is a group of one ritual status, 'one blood', a concept implying descent from a common ancestor, but the *pavula* is also a group which acts together, and here the sanction for co-operation stems from the obligations inherent in marriage alliance. The *pavula* is formed on the twin principles of common descent—implying equal ritual status—and marriage—implying co-operation.

Of course, in this system, marriage relations do not stand in sharp contrast to blood kinship. Kinsmen by marriage and descent are often one and the same. Kandyan Sinhalese do not use separate terms for these 'categories' of kin—both are merely *nādäyo* (kinsmen). This reflects the fact that most marriages are between persons already related by descent; blood relations are thus constantly turned into relations by marriage. Hence the *pavula* can be regarded as groups of kinsmen related by blood, who are further bound together by alliances of marriage which intertwine and connect the entire group.

Both the notion of common descent, connected as it is with ritual status, and the desire for close co-operation in marriage alliances, contribute to a preference for close endogamous marriages.

We have noted the role of property in marriage alliances. Women carry potential claims on land and cash, but the management of a woman's property is largely in the hands of her male relations. It is then the men's concern to ensure that the property 'must not go out'. The strategy of marriage alliances is therefore to arrange either that the women of the *pavula* are married to close kinsmen within the *pavula* or else that such strangers as are allowed to marry the women of the *pavula* should themselves be incorporated into the *pavula*. In either case a centripetal tendency is evident. The marriage pattern is, by its very nature, turned inward.

But note further: since 'outsiders' who become husbands to women of the *pavula* must themselves be incorporated into the *pavula* it is necessary to ensure that both they and their kinsmen are acceptable on grounds of ritual status as well as of wealth. When marriages are being arranged the first question to be raised by the *pavula* kinsmen is that of *jāti*—that is 'caste' in the sense of ritual status within the caste as a whole.

The ritual status of close kin carries immediate implications regarding one's own. All members of the *pavula* are necessarily of the same ritual status, for, as outsiders would say, 'these people eat together, they have intermarried, they are one blood'. Hence the entire *pavula* is directly interested in the marriages of *all* its members. Its ritual status is 'contained' in both its men and women; it must be safeguarded in both sexes. In case of a 'wrong' marriage, the culprit, and all those who might support him (or her) and continue to interdine with him would have to be 'excommunicated'. [8] The marriages of both men and women must, therefore, be confined to 'acceptable' people. The problem is two-sided: (*a*) 'low' affines must not be allowed into the kin group, and (*b*) the parentage of the offspring of any member of the *pavula* must be 'clean' so that they may, in their turn, be marriageable to the offspring of the rest of the *pavula*. For the ritual status of the *pavula* is conveyed from generation to generation by both its male and female members.

Thus both from considerations of property and co-operation and also with a view to ritual status there is the tendency to keep marriages within narrow ranges. Bilateral kinship spreads far and wide, but close endogamous marriage reinforces kinship ties, furthers the sense of dependence on kinsmen, keeps property in 'reliable', 'close' circles and, above all, safeguards the ritual qualities in the blood of the 'kindred'.

Marriage choices

The tendency towards endogamy does not then arise from any 'law' or custom imposed from above by caste councils; it is the result of preferences. The father of a girl has a choice in what he does with her. There are certain occasions when it may be desirable to look outside the *pavula* circle for a marriage. For example, a particular parent may discover that all his close kinsmen are poorer than himself. He may then decide to look for affinal relatives as wealthy as himself. Alternatively, a person of low rank who has made his fortune may decide that he would prefer to acquire affinal kin of high birth (and/or superior influence) rather than wealthy relatives.

The first choice is not so difficult and in Terutenne most marriages were between people of comparable wealth in land or money. There was a tendency to 'break' kinship with those relatives who were not very close kin (e.g. first and second cousins) and who were poorer than oneself.

The second choice, however, is complicated. Let us note, immediately, that all marriages between persons of differing ritual status are expected to be hypergamous. I do not wish to go into the reasons for this expectation in this context. It is sufficient to observe that the sexual association of 'good' women, of 'good' ancestry and titles, with 'bad' men—even though they be of the same caste—is considered to be very reprehensible indeed. Such unions are extremely rare. [9]

On the other hand, it is possible for a daughter to be married *up* the ritual hierarchy (in the same caste) to a man of superior ritual status. In that case, however, financial sacrifice on the part of the girl's father becomes absolutely essential. No man can expect to acquire a son-in-law who is both of higher ritual status than himself and also of equal wealth, for any such potential son-in-law could always find a father-in-law of equal wealth and equal status to himself. Therefore the aspiring father-in-law, if he insists upon social climbing in this fashion, can get himself a son-in-law of higher ritual status only if he is prepared to accept a man who is inferior in wealth.

Such choices are to be expected in a community such as Terutenne which is highly differentiated both in ritual status (*vangsa*, *jāti*) and in wealth. Since a rise in one scale does not automatically entail a corresponding rise in the other, the attempt to convert wealth into ritual status is understandable.

Marriage is the best method of effecting this conversion, but the greater the divergence in social position between the parties, the greater the financial sacrifice which is called for. Alternatively, if wealth is to be maximized, then the best choice for both father-in-law and son-in-law is to seek a partner at the same status level. A man can acquire relatives who are his equals *both* in wealth *and* in ritual status only by remaining orthodox. Thus paradoxically, it is because wealth is greatly valued that men prefer to marry not only within the same caste but also within the same status level within the same caste.

Much the same argument would apply also to cross-caste unions. A very rich low-caste woman can always obtain a high-caste consort. But neither she nor her children will thereby become high-caste. Nor would her kin stand to gain very much from the union. Hence there is little temptation on either side to enter into cross-caste unions. It is then clear that, in Terutenne, the caste divisions themselves as well as the gradations within the castes are preserved not because of any law but because of the self-interest of individuals. The caste barriers are not 'categorical imperatives' sanctioned by direct communal force, but are the cumulative result of individual decisions. Let us now turn to the connexions—such as they are—between the castes.

3. Intercaste unions

> We know what fate falls
> On families broken:
> The rites are forgotten,
> Vice rots the remnant
> Defiling the *women*
> And from *their* corruption
> Comes mixing of castes:
> The curse of confusion... (my italics).
>
> *Bhagavad-Gita*: The Sorrow of Arjuna
> (Prabhavananda 1947: 36).

In the literature on India there is frequent mention of intercaste 'marriages'. The nature of such 'marriage' is often ambiguous. For instance, the Nayar–Nambudiri *sambandam* is regarded as 'marriage' by Hutton (1946: 47, 136), whereas the Nambudiri themselves make a clear distinction between unions in which the husband and wife are both Nambudiri Brahmans, and those others in which Nambudiri men have liaisons with Nayar women. The children inherit Nambudiri Brahman property in the former case only, in the latter the visiting Nambudiri man may neither eat with his Nayar concubine, nor even—after a bath—touch her or his children (Gough 1955: 48).

We must therefore distinguish between three separate forms of regular connexions (cf. Leach 1955).

(1) Regularized sexual liaisons.

(2) The establishment of domestic, conjugal and commensal unions.

(3) The *alliance* between kinsmen, with the implication that it be perpetuated in the next generation.

The people of Terutenne, together with many other Kandyan peasants, often dispensed with marriage ceremonies altogether and set up house without any formalities. It was then not an easy matter to distinguish between mere sexual intercourse, concubinage and accepted marriage. The term *sambanda* may cover all three types of relationship and if a man is having an affair with a woman of his own caste it may well be difficult to decide exactly what the relationship is. Such a woman may be referred to as *pavula* (wife) and then, if the relations tend to become permanent, it may be said that the man has 'married' (*pavula una* or *kasāda bända*).

In the meantime, however, he or she may have been excommunicated by the rest of the family. In that case, while the first or second aspects of the 'union' (sexual or domestic union) may be established, the *alliance* is conspicuous by its absence. Hence, in *kinship* terms, a true marriage does not exist.

If, in such cases, the woman and the man are of different caste, then the woman will not even be referred to as *pavula* (wife) but merely as *gāni* (woman) and normally—but not invariably—a public domestic union would not be established. A full-scale *alliance* would here be out of the question.

Let us analyse this situation. It should be recalled that, from the point of view of the 'kindred', the essence of the matter is the preservation of ritual purity, mainly in the 'blood', but also, to a lesser extent, in terms of food and sexual intercourse.

But although eating with low-caste persons is polluting, the pollution can be cleansed by certain accepted methods. Hence, unless it becomes a habit, the culprit need not be outcasted. In Terutenne, many of my high-caste friends did not mind sitting down in private to a meal with some rich Blacksmiths even though the Blacksmiths had helped in the cooking. This would be vehemently denied in public.

The same can be said about sexual intercourse between a high-caste man and a low-caste woman. As Stevenson (1954) observes, it is here only the man who is 'polluted' and he can then take a bath and return to a state of 'purity'.

The reverse case is different. It has always been emphasized, even from ancient times, that high-caste women must not have intercourse with low-caste men on pain of death. This is clearly stated in the Laws of Manu where *anuloma* ('with the hair', i.e. high man, low woman) and *pratiloma* ('against the hair', i.e. low man, high woman) unions are distinguished (Hutton 1946: 48).

And Robert Knox, the famous prisoner in the Kandyan kingdom in the seventeenth century, writes as follows:

And if any of the Females should be so deluded, as to commit Folly with one beneath herself...they would certainly kill her, there being no other way to wipe off the dishonour she hath done the Family, but by her own Blood.

Yet for the men it is different; it is not accounted any shame or fault for a Man of the highest sort to lay with a Woman far inferiour to himself, nay of the very lowest degree; provided he neither eats nor drinks with her, nor takes her home to his House, as a Wife.

Neither do they reckon their Wives to be Whores for lying with them that are as good or better than themselves.

(Knox 1911: 105, 148; cf. Ryan 1953: 153–4; D'Oyly 1929: 180; Pieris 1956: 178.)

What is the reason for this distinction? Stevenson (1954) is of the opinion that the woman is 'internally' polluted by the low-caste person and this is more difficult to cleanse than 'external' pollution. But there are other aspects to the matter. In the case of a high-caste man having an affair with a low-caste woman, the question of the caste affiliation of the possible offspring does not seriously arise. If the woman has children, they will remain with her and—under normal conditions—will remain in her family and caste.

But the position is different in the case of a liaison between a high-caste woman and a low-caste man, for then the woman's offspring would be polluted 'in their blood'.

To eliminate the pollution from the mother's kin group three possible procedures might be adopted:

(1) The children could be classed as belonging solely to the low caste of the father, but this would imply separation of the children from the mother at birth, which is hardly practical.

(2) The mother and her children could be destroyed. This was the classical norm—death by drowning for mother and child alike.

(3) The mother and her children could be excommunicated from their caste to prevent the pollution from spreading further through later inter-marriage within the *pavula*. This is the correct procedure at the present time.

This bias, which imposes more rigorous sex rules upon women than upon men, demonstrates that, while ritual status is transmitted through both men and women and must be safeguarded in both sexes, maternal filiation is given greater significance than the paternal connexion. In my view, it is because of the possible consequences for potential offspring that in this society hyper-gamous sex relations may be tolerated, but hypogamous relations are absolutely repudiated.

Hypogamy apart, the people of Terutenne paid little attention to extra-marital sex relations, even when the parties were of different caste. Many high-caste men had passing liaisons with low-caste women. The children of such unions belonged, in every case, to the mother's kin group.

All these men repudiated 'eating' with the women, thus bearing out Stevenson's observations. In the opinion of the men, interdining with 'low' women was worse than sleeping with them.

There were two cases only in the whole village in which public domestic unions had been established between men and women of differing castes. In one a beautiful Potter girl had induced a man from another district—who claimed with some success to be of the Radala, the most exalted section of the Goyigama—to settle with her. He was himself very poor. He both lived with her and ate her food. His position in the village was anomalous (see p. 86).

The other case, also a love match, concerned a Tom-tom Beater and a Washer-girl. The girl's family were particularly incensed and attempted to kill the 'husband'. Here it might perhaps be thought that since *both* the man and the woman were 'low', there would be no reason to refrain from inter-marriage. But in fact the *respective* status of the low castes is a matter of potential dispute. This 'marriage' if recognized would have implied that the Washermen were 'lower' than the Tom-tom Beaters (see pp. 83, 84).

We see then that, while hypogamous unions of all kinds are ruled out, cross-caste sex relations are not considered particularly objectionable so long as the relationship is hypergamous. It needs to be understood, however, that such hypergamous cross-caste liaisons can never be recognized as alliances between kin groups. For the alliance carries the implication of kinship (*nākama*), of commensality, and of conjugality. By interdining, the two kin groups which are parties to the alliance acquire 'equal' status, and in recognizing their mutual kinship they imply that further marriage ties will be appropriate in the future.

It is worth noting that the argument I have outlined here is broadly in line with that of the classical authorities on Kandyan customary law who, in general, confined the term 'marriage' to mean what I have here called an 'alliance'.

Sawers' *Digest of Kandyan Law* contains the following:

What constitutes a regular marriage is as follows:

The Consent of the respective Heads of families; the countenance and sanction of the Relations to the third or fourth degree on both sides, to the union of the parties, that they must be of the same Caste and of equal family, respectability and rank which is chiefly ascertained by the families having previously intermarried....

The near relations have the right to object to the Parent's (*sic*) disposing of their Daughter in an unequal match, that would be considered discreditable to the other connexions.... (D'Oyly 1929: 127, 129.)

Where this consent is not forthcoming, then—in my terminology—the alliance is not established and the relationship is either concubinage or merely clandestine sex relationship. The absence of a formal alliance does not in itself make the children illegitimate unless there is a public act of excommunication.

There was no penalty against concubinage, if the woman was of equal caste with the man—but in fact such connections if not stigmatized by some decisive act on the part of the man's family, or by the man himself, were considered as marriages, and the issue of such connections have all the privileges of legitimate children. In short, nothing but a direct declaration of disinheriting such issue would cut them off.... (D'Oyly 1929: 130; the quotation comes from Sawers' *Digest*.)

For these early authorities an 'intercaste *marriage*' would have been a contradiction in terms since all 'carnal conversation between the sexes of different castes is penal' (*op. cit.* p. 130), though it was only a technical offence if the man was of the higher caste. Even so, in certain specified instances, a man of high caste, who lacked close relations, could transfer property, especially movable property, to his children by a woman of lower caste (cf. Pieris 1956: 202–3). It is clear that the children in question remained in their mother's caste and that no cross-caste alliance could be established by this concession. The implication of such rules was (and is) that however often individual men establish 'concubinage relationships' across caste boundaries, the ideology of 'caste purity' and 'caste endogamy' is preserved because the caste outsider is not recognized as an affinal kinsman.

Today the legal position is considerably more confused than it was in the days of Sawers and D'Oyly. Individuals may enter into registered legal marriages without the consent of their kinsmen and the caste of the parties concerned is of no legal consequence (*K.M.D.A.* 1952: 5 f.). Consequently, it is possible for there to be an intercaste union which is a valid marriage in the eyes of the law, but which, on account of caste difference or excommunication, is not a valid marriage alliance in terms of custom. Yet the children of this same intercaste union may have a perfectly 'legitimate' customary status in the caste group of their mother. The law, which does not recognize caste, asserts that the children of any registered marriage are the lawful children of both parents, but custom, which recognizes caste, specifies that the children can belong to one caste only and not two. Custom recognizes the union of the parents but not the alliance between their kinsmen, thus the basic principle of caste purity is preserved.

I have been at pains to emphasize that in the village of Terutenne *alliances* are not established across caste lines. There are some exceptions to this statement which—in my opinion—prove the rule. These concern 'outsiders' who enter Terutenne society as complete strangers.

Caste status is something which is made public by certain criteria and symbols. Anyone who can confuse the criteria and change the symbols, can alter his caste status. Outsiders are in an admirable position in this respect. If their kinship connexions are unknown, and if they choose not to state their caste, then by changing their caste-linked name and occupations they can pretend to be anything they fancy. And they can get away with it.

In theory no one should countenance intermarriage with a 'stranger'. The presumption is always that such a man is of low caste. But in practice an outsider who can make a show of wealth or influence often finds it possible to persuade a local family to accept him as a son-in-law. Even high-caste wives may be obtained in this way. Such unions are not merely hypogamous, they are alliances. The high-caste kinsmen of the wife pretend, even when they know the facts to be otherwise, that their new relative is of the same high caste as themselves.

In Terutenne, in 1955, there were at least a dozen households in which the husband was of Low Country origin. Most of them had originally settled there as traders. Some were said to be Christians of the Karāva (fisher) caste. Low Country Karāva names such as Eva Fransea Perera, Marie Antoinette, Don Juan de Silva, Andradi Antoni were in fact common among them.

The mother of Fransea was an old woman. She was a native of Terutenne and still retained her Kandyan name Mutumenika. Years ago she married a Karāva husband and she described to me the pomp and splendour of her Christian wedding in a nearby town. But after the death of her husband she had reverted to Buddhism and her children likewise.

It is typical of such outsider householders that they become assimilated to the local population. A school teacher with whom I was on good terms told me the following details of his life history.

He had originally been a Karāva Christian. He had worked in a bazaar in the Kandyan Hills doing all kinds of menial tasks. He had saved money and educated himself and finally become a school teacher. Some time later he had seen the truth of Buddha's teaching and ceased to attend churches. He had one sister but no other relative living in the Kandyan Hills. He succeeded in marrying off his sister to an aristocratic family in Terutenne. These people were poor Goyigama and found it useful to have this connexion with a salaried Government servant. Later the schoolmaster himself married a Kandyan woman and had many children by her. These children were given names from Indian mythology. Their father, who was an accomplished astrologer, found that their horoscopes forbade them ever to go near the sea. The schoolmaster had worked in different schools in various parts of the district but he had purchased land in Terutenne which had been cultivated by his affinal relatives. Eventually he himself retired in Terutenne together with his family.

In 1955 negotiations were afoot regarding the marriages of his children. Two of his daughters had married very rich Karāva boutique-keepers in the same anomalous position as himself, but another daughter had been given to his sister's son to renew the Goyigama alliance. In this fashion, having once been a Karāva Christian, he had now become a Buddhist Goyigama.

Much of this story was well known and well publicized by his enemies in the village. But since he already had large numbers of local relatives through his sister and his wife, all of whom were of impeccable Goyigama descent, the attacks did him little harm. In any case, in the next generation no one would be able to disentangle the facts of kinship from the myths.

Cases of this sort are important, for they elucidate the very essence of caste. There are four main reasons why it is possible for men like the schoolmaster to break through caste barriers:

(1) They are not of the locality; caste is local.

(2) They start without local kinship connexions: caste is demonstrated by kinship.

(3) They have repudiated their former caste occupations: caste is related to occupation.

(4) They have changed their names: caste is indicated by traditional names.

I have referred to these cases of caste transfer as the negative instances which prove the rule: for, although individuals penetrate through caste barriers, they do not disturb them and, indeed, they reaffirm, by their behaviour, the essential principles which perpetuate the ideology of caste.

To recapitulate the findings of this section: I have described how the individual Kandyan has a choice about his marriages. Caste endogamy is not enforced upon him by organized courts. Granted the ideology of a special quality residing in the blood, his actions—motivated by self-interest—tend to uphold caste 'endogamy'. The role of Kandyan kinship is crucial here, for it is the emphasis on marriage as an alliance of kinship—to be perpetuated in the next generation—which produces a tendency towards endogamy within the kin group (*pavula*).

Intercaste 'marriages' are illusory. Within the village, where the affiliations of all individuals are well known, intercaste unions do not go further than 'hypergamous' concubinage or copulation. The children follow maternal affiliation. If, on the other hand, the relations are 'hypogamous' then the culprits are dealt with by excommunication from the *pavula*. And in this fashion ritual status is preserved, for no polluted persons can enter the group.

When 'strangers' are involved in intercaste unions, their 'lowness' and pollution is denied. Hence, by the very denial, the principle of caste purity is reaffirmed.

RITUAL STATUS

1. *The 'low' castes*

In the last section we considered the reasons which made each *pavula* family partly and each caste community entirely endogamous. In so doing, I treated the dogma of ritual status as one of the unchangeable *a priori* concepts in the total scheme. It was in the nature of things that certain names, occupations and localities carried the connotation of high or low ritual status in a sense which hardly needed further definition.

This is an over-simplification. Caste (ritual) status is not always immutably fixed. For India, Professor Srinivas has given descriptions of communities improving their hereditary status positions by carefully adopting ways of behaviour—of dress, and habits and religion—which have been associated with 'purity' since time immemorial (1952: 31, 35; also Cohn 1955: *passim*).

This section is concerned with the principles which perpetuate ritual status while at the same time allowing for changes to take place in the ranking of particular communities and individuals.

We have already considered the general position and constitution of 'low'-caste communities in Terutenne, but we must now turn back and ask ourselves why these 'low' castes are 'low'; why are Blacksmiths and Potters 'low' and why are the individual carpenters or boutique-keepers not 'low'?

The 'lowness' of communities depends on a combination of three elements: (a) traditional names, (b) occupation, (c) communal distinction.

(a) The 'lowness' of caste names

Caste names such as Āchāri, Baddē, Hēna and so on are themselves part of an elaborate tradition which specifies that these are low castes of low occupation which have always been low. Belief in this tradition is not simply part of the dogma of Goyigama superiority. The lowness of the low caste is thought to be a natural fact on which even the low castes themselves—at least in Terutenne—are agreed (cf. Cohn 1955: 61). To demonstrate the extreme potency attributed to the caste name as such, I may mention the case of the Rodiyā, the lowest of all the Kandyan castes. A proposal made by the Kandyan Peasantry Commission with a view to improving the social standing of these unfortunates was that the Government should 'remove the *word Rodiyā* by legislation' (*R.K.P.C.* 483, my italics). And indeed there is a genuine sense in which one might say that a caste without a name could have no defined ritual status.

(b) The 'lowness' of caste occupations

In some cases, for example that of the Washerman, it is easy to see how the traditional occupation of a particular caste group has come to be classed as 'low' and 'polluting', but this is not always the case. Logical explanations can be produced to show why Blacksmiths and Potters and Tom-tom Beaters can be said to be 'pursuing a polluting occupation'. But such rationalizations do not really explain the facts. Whatever the original logic of the case, the traditions of centuries have indelibly associated these particular occupations with particular positions in the ritual hierarchy. The lowness of certain occupations permeates the entire superstructure of traditional beliefs, rituals and sentiments (cf. Srinivas 1955(b): 21–2).

In terms of traditional occupation the Goyigama are the cultivators. But in fact all castes engage in cultivation. Farming is not a *special* occupation at all. In contrast, Tom-tom Beaters and Jaggory-makers pursue traditional callings which are peculiar to themselves. The former have institutional roles in temples and on annual ceremonies, and the latter carry certain foodstuffs to weddings. Even where there are none to perform these tasks, it is known that they fall to the lot of 'special' people, and no respectable person would perform such service in public.

Working for others and especially the acceptance of cash payment are vaguely felt to place one in an inferior position. The castes which are paid for services which none other would perform demonstrate the truth of this notion. They are 'low' because they work for others and they work for others because they are 'born' low. Hence the low castes may collectively be spoken of as 'the working people' (*väda karani minissu*), not only by the high-caste but by themselves.

But as between the various 'low' castes in Terutenne, there was no agreement on ritual status. Being entirely separate communities, each one considered itself to be 'better' than the others. And this provided an extra reason for avoiding all intermarriage with the others, since the community which consented to give women would *ipso facto* have to admit that it was of lower rank. The Goyigama, of course, are uninterested in the mutual pretensions to status among the low-caste groups.

(c) The 'lowness' of communal distinction

The fact that the castes are entirely distinct endogamous communities made it feasible and understandable to speak of their 'collective status'.

'But the Hēna used to wash clothes for all my ancestors and their ancestors.'

'The Tom-tom Beaters always work in the temples: they are all low. They are all related.'

One reason why the carpenters did not constitute a caste group was that they did not form a closed community which could be directly indicated. There were no traditions in Terutenne which associated them by name or occupation with low ritual position.

It is interesting that many of the low castes mentioned by ancient writers seem to have disappeared (Ryan 1953: ch. III, *passim*). The most likely explanation is that they have disappeared by merging with other castes. This may be due to economic factors. Most of the 'low' castes of today derive a distinct material benefit from the exercise of their caste services. All the four low castes in Terutenne had remunerative traditional occupations.

It is difficult to assess the value of such remuneration as a factor tending to the perpetuation of caste grouping. Many low-caste individuals in Terutenne had never learnt and therefore could not practise their traditional caste occupation.

Thus, in the case of the Tom-tom Beaters, I estimate that ten professional drummers and dancers would have sufficed for all the temple services. But the Tom-tom Beater community numbered 146 individuals in all. Most of the men were landless and worked as wage-labourers on the fields of others. Any individual member of this 'surplus' population of Tom-tom Beaters was free to leave the neighbourhood and sever his local caste and kinship connexions. But no one showed any inclination to do so. Consequently so long as they remained in Terutenne, absolutely connected to a named, marked community, their status persisted. They remained 'low-caste Tom-tom Beaters' whether they knew how to drum or not.

Such resigned acceptance of an inferior status will seem strange to many European readers, but it should be remembered that the basic tenets of the religious system entirely support it. In Buddhism as in Hinduism the emphasis is on resignation, on right behaviour, and on the renunciation of worldly ambition.

In considering the ranking of the low castes it is important to distinguish between economic class and ritual status. The Blacksmiths of Terutenne provide an illustration of this distinction. They were among the richest people in the whole village and had large holdings of paddy land. At the same time their traditional occupation as blacksmiths continued to provide a major source of income. The Blacksmiths are wealthy but they cannot escape from their low ritual status without abandoning their traditional occupation, which would be costly. Again there is the question of kinship. Any individual Blacksmith family which chose to climb out of the low-caste status of Blacksmith would have to renounce all its kinship links with other Blacksmiths. The advantages to be gained from social climbing are not really very tempting!

So much for questions of status among the low castes. I conclude that in Terutenne the place of low castes in the hierarchy is fixed and that there is no evidence of castes having recently succeeded in changing their collective status as communities. What 'fixes' them are the traditional names, occupations and communal distinctions. These, I think, are the 'identification marks' of the low castes. Anyone who can be demonstrably shown to have such 'identification marks' is 'low'. Those individuals who can succeed in ridding themselves of these 'marks' may have success in caste climbing, but this is not an ambition which in fact appeals to many people.

2. Ranking among the Goyigama

In discussing the low castes, attention was drawn to three distinguishing criteria: names, occupations, communal distinctions. I now want to consider a fourth criterion: place of residence.

This factor, which does not seem very important in the case of the low castes—they are sufficiently clearly marked by names and occupations—assumes much greater significance among Goyigama: for Kandyans frequently refer to whole villages as 'low' in the same fashion as they do to 'communities'. The implications of 'locality' as a mark of identification will become clear in the following pages.

We have noted that with the 'low' castes wealth and influence and traditional caste position do not need to correspond. Blacksmiths are wealthy but 'low' because they are Āchāri and because they engage in a demeaning traditional calling. Goyigama may be poor but they are always of high ritual status.

A sharp distinction between the symbols of secular and of ritual status is not confined to caste systems. It may be considered normal for all priest-hoods. Christian monks, Buddhist priests, Brahman hermits all have high ritual status which is specifically associated with an ideal of poverty. But among secular commoners we usually find that the possession of wealth and influence is consistent with the holding of high ritual status and that this 'highness' is associated with the adoption of specific symbolic attributes—top hats for example! Change in total status may then be associated with change in symbolic 'identification marks'.

I shall describe two such cases. The first concerns a named locality, traditionally the home of 'low' serfs, and I shall show how the 'low name' has come to taint the status of recent immigrants to the locality. The second describes the manœuvres of a 'low' family which, having acquired wealth and influence, succeeded in shaking off its 'low' name in favour of aristocratic titles. In both cases the 'low' and 'high' groups are alike Goyigama.

(a) Gālpitiya

I have already described the traditional ranking of the Goyigama in Teru-tenne. 'In the days of the Sinhalese Kings'—that period when people behaved in the 'correct' fashion—the high caste was divided into three broad layers. First were the aristocratic houses who owned most of the land; second came the ordinary high-caste people owing only allegiance and nominal service; and lastly the 'serfs' who worked for the aristocratic houses in return for certain lands and free house sites. My first example is concerned with the status of these 'lowest' people.

When I first settled in Terutenne, it became immediately clear that the place was subdivided into smaller *named* residential groups, which I refer to as hamlets.

Their reputations were markedly different. Looking across the valley, the local youths would point to a hamlet halfway up the hillside in a clump of trees and say 'That place, Gālpitiya, is very low birth (*pahat jāti*): we have nothing to do with them.' 'Why?' I would ask, 'You work on the same lands: and they come here frequently—are they not Goyigama?' 'Yes, they are Goyigama but 99% good, 1% bad; we do not take any food or drink from them and do not exchange women with them.' And they would explain that 'in those days' they were 'working people'.

It should be recalled that feudal services were abolished in the last century and whatever their past position in the social system such 'low people' were not—strictly speaking—'serfs' at all. They could not have been forced to labour and such lands or gardens as they possessed belonged to themselves and not to aristocratic overlords.

Even so, in the rest of Terutenne, as well as in other villages in the Walapane district where the 'myth' of the servile past of the hamlet was still alive,

Gālpitiya was held in contempt. Though admitted to be of the Goyigama high caste, and therefore quite different from the 'true' low castes, the people of Gālpitiya were not entitled to respect. They would not be offered chairs in other Goyigama houses and it was claimed that respectable villagers would neither eat their food not drink their water. These people of Gālpitiya had no specific caste name nor any specific caste occupation. Hence they did not possess the most potent 'identification marks' of low status. They were merely an interrelated group of people to whom tradition attached the myth of servile descent (see also Ryan 1953: 217 ff.).

Here lies the interest of Gālpitiya: it has the makings of 'caste'—the assertion of ritual status, the claims about endogamy and social intercourse—yet it is not a 'caste' for it cannot be identified with any of the traditional divisions of the Goyigama. It was merely a local sub-group within the Goyigama community in Terutenne.

Gālpitiya was not entirely alone in its predicament. The same claims were made about other hamlets in the district. Anyone who lived in one of these places was tainted with the ritual status of the hamlet unless he could produce convincing evidence to the contrary.

Many of these 'low' hamlets had names ending in -*pitiya* (place). Gālpitiya was merely one of these. Indeed the whole name had some unpleasant implications, meaning 'the place of cattle'. The inhabitants strongly disliked this name and they grumbled that 'Gālpitiya is a wrong name; we don't know why this place is called like that'. When I asked the 'real' name, I would be told, 'Oh! we searched the temple here. You know it was all in ruins until *Kiriunga* (the rich washerman) had it rebuilt and at that time we found ancient documents in the temple. The real name is Karandamaditta.' The rest of Terutenne had neither heard of, nor cared to know, the name Karandamaditta.

There are two questions here which are of interest. First: granted that the people of Gālpitiya are 'low' today, is the historical explanation—that they are low because they are the 'descendants of serfs'—to be accepted? Second: is this explanation true? Are the people of Gālpitiya really descended from 'serfs'?

To answer the latter question first: I had access to certain historical documents about Terutenne—grain tithe registers which were kept from about 1830 to 1895 and which indicated the ownership of all paddy land in the village throughout that period. [10] They showed the 'low' status of Gālpitiya in two respects. First, the names of Gālpitiya people were different from those of ordinary villagers. All the 'good' Goyigama in Terutenne have 'ancestral titles' (*vasagama*) and 'house names' (*gedara nāma*) before their personal names (Pieris 1956: 172 ff.). Both symbolize superior rank. In the past those who worked as 'serfs' did not have 'ancestral titles' or 'hereditary names'. They were not allowed to use them and the usurpation of such titles would have been punishable offences.

At the present time the aristocrats have little power, and name changing is not 'illegal'. Many 'low' people have therefore invented exquisite and chivalrous titles for themselves (cf. Carstairs 1957: 59). The registers, on the other hand, showed the state of affairs during the nineteenth century. At that time, although most of the villagers had titles and house names, the inhabitants of the 'low' hamlet were simply recorded as, for instance, 'Banda of Gāl-pitiya (*Gālpitiya Banda*)'. The registers also showed that the sum total of paddy land which belonged to the people of Gālpitiya was minute compared to the large estates of the lordly families. [11] It seems probable then that tradition is correct and that Gālpitiya was in fact inhabited by people of low rank for a long time.

Let me now turn to the second question. Granted that the hamlet was inhabited by servile people in the past, is this an explanation of why the people in Gālpitiya are still 'low' to this day? Is Gālpitiya 'low' merely because its past is marred? Why should the 'past' continue to set this hamlet apart even though serfdom is abolished, and even though the inhabitants do not form a named and recognized subcaste?

Here tradition is at fault. The inhabitants of Gālpitiya, far from being the descendants of its past inhabitants, were newcomers. Some time at the beginning of this century, when the government were resettling landless families on new colonization schemes, there had been a *complete* change in the population of Gālpitiya. All the actual descendants of past serfs left the locality and gradually new people of diverse origin resettled the hamlet.

True, there had been no definite break. The newcomers had settled gradually. And according to strict caste theory even if only very few of them had intermarried with the original inhabitants, these newcomers would have been tainted, and it could be claimed that pollution had spread to the whole community as they intermarried—like some kind of smallpox.

But this kind of explanation was not used. The fact is that, while in Gālpitiya itself almost every family had a distinct tradition of having arrived from somewhere else, the rest of Terutenne was entirely uninterested in the matter.

There is, however, a further aspect of Gālpitiya status and this relates to wealth. Although paddy land is the most valuable property in any dry-zone village, shifting cultivation is also practised. In Terutenne whole families could—if necessary—live entirely by shifting cultivation. In 1955 annual permits for shifting cultivation were not difficult to acquire but irrigated paddy land was extremely scarce. Much of the latter was owned by rich land-lords. The villagers who had little or no paddy land of their own could work either as wage-labourers or as share-croppers on the lands of the rich. [12]

Gālpitiya contained the poorest people in the whole village. Apart from two dwelling groups (which owned 10 *pāla* between them) the entire population had only 7 *pāla* in aggregate. This may be compared with the average holdings for the whole village and with the holdings of the rich landlords, as shown in Table 4.

Table 4. *Paddy land holdings*

	Total population	Total paddy land (*pāla*)	Percentage of total paddy land	Average per head
Terutenne (whole village)	1192	592	100	0·49
Gālpitiya (excluding 2 wealthy dwelling groups)	141	7	0·8	0·06
Terutenne: households of 16 wealthiest landlords, each with holdings larger than 7 *pāla*	91	242	40·8	2·60

Yet Gālpitiya was not 'low' simply because it was poor. Many other Goyigama, who lived elsewhere, were just as poor in terms of paddy land, but were not considered 'low' at all. The 'badness' of Gālpitiya people was derived from a simple principle of association. They lived in a locality to which tradition assigned servile status. Like the original inhabitants they, too, had little paddy land. They, too, worked on the fields of others—though no longer under an obligation to do so. But the essentials had not changed: Gālpitiya, which had been a fund of labouring serfs in the ancient kingdom, remained a fund of labourers.

(b) The assumption of hereditary titles

Having indicated how traditions are attached to named localities and how these are considered to be 'identification marks' of ritual status, I turn to the use of 'titles' (see also Ryan 1953: 318-19).

It was only a few hours after I arrived in Terutenne that I found all the enemies of the local ruling 'clique' ready to explain to me the quite deplorable ancestry of 'those' people. I remained there ten months and the enemies never gave up. They claimed that some of the richest and most influential persons in Terutenne were descended from 'serfs'. These 'serfs' had arrived from Dehi Gaha Pitiya—a few miles away—some time at the turn of the century. They had at first lived in some nearby caves and subsisted by shifting cultivation. Their manners and customs were atrocious. They were like Veddahs! One of them, Kalu Banda, had eventually succeeded in getting hold of an aristocratic woman from Tun Amunu Gedara. She had been excommunicated, but the harm was done.

After this incident, on which most people agreed, the story of the Dehi Gaha Pitiya people is one of resounding success. Luck had been on their side. The Government Agent of the time had been a keen elephant hunter, and the father of Kalu Banda used to act as a guide. On one occasion, as a wild elephant charged the Government Agent, whose rifle refused to fire, Kalu Banda's father had saved his life by killing the elephant with a single shot. The grateful Agent had presented Kalu Banda's father with an inscribed gun —which, indeed, was shown to me with considerable family pride.

This fund of good-will at the apex of the official hierarchy was put to good use. Kalu Banda's famly had laid a dark plot against the ruling village head-man of the time. They had succeeded in persuading the European officials that the headman was mixed up in a complex affair, involving a murder and kidnapping, on which my informants dwelt with fascination. The result had been the dismissal of the headman and the succession of Dehi Gaha Pitiya Kalu Banda [13] to the post of village headman.

The headmanship had provided new sources of income. Kalu Banda, the new village headman, began to use the aristocratic titles of his wife. To make the process secure, he took yet another woman from the same family and, hence, had *two* wives with the same titles. Naturally all his sons, too, assumed their maternal titles. But this was not all. A little later two of Kalu Banda's brothers also married women from the *same* aristocratic house and assumed the same titles. Eventually, not only their descendants, but many of their kinsmen—their sisters' sons and daughters and their children—all assumed the high ranking name of Nissanka Mudiyansēlāgē Tun Amunu Gedara. [13]

When I was in the village they were normally only referred to as the Nissanka or Tun Amunu clique, but never openly as Dehi Gaha Pitiya. I was made to realize the power and connotations of these names when I saw the great concern—indeed fear—in the faces of people who related the story to me in utmost secrecy. There could have been no joking about it.

The authenticity of these incidents may be doubted. I can only state that after ten months in Terutenne, I became utterly convinced of their truth. Moreover, there was an occasion when two members of this Nissanka clique became involved in a case of infanticide. Both of them had been keeping the same young concubine, but both tried to shirk the responsibility for the girl's pregnancy. The infant was eventually found dead and, in the courts, the mother accused both her lovers of murder and they, in turn, accused each other. One of these men came to me for help. In his hatred against his own kinsman, he made me write down the entire history of the rise of the Nissanka clique from low Dehi Gaha to the splendid Nissanka Mudiansēlāgē Tun Amunu Gedara. In doing so, he threw all the responsibility for certain shady incidents—even the name-changing—on to his other kinsmen. He had only followed them, and they were the 'guilty' ones.

None the less, their present titles were a fitting façade to their acquired but impressive affluence. They covered the unpleasant ancestry most effectively. Despite the libellous gossip even their worst enemies would have hesitated to bring the matter up in public. And while the façade remained, backed by solid wealth, other aristocratic families—especially those who were less wealthy—encouraged intermarriage with the 'upstarts'. Hence, with the passage of time, they acquired an ever-widening circle of 'respectable' kinsmen.

These incidents are the reverse of the Gālpitiya case. There, the name and locality had been associated with 'low' status. When the old families of 'ex-serfs' left the village, the locality was once again occupied by poor and unimportant people. Hence there was no incongruity between tradition and present fact. In the case of the Dehi Gaha Pitiya, wealth and influence were in blatant contrast to their traditional status. Hence, the switch-over in the titles—the assumption of titles through women—had made their ritual status consistent with their actual power.

I have drawn attention to the economic and political factors behind the changes in ritual status. But, let us note that the 'names' are at the very heart of the matter. It is these epithets, or symbols, or 'identification marks' which must be altered, for they are the instruments whereby individuals and communities are 'placed' in the hierarchy.

Names and titles are not, of course, the only 'identification marks': occupations or localities ('so and so village is low!') may serve the purpose as well. If all these can be modified, and if some 'higher' people can be persuaded to accept a marriage, then, in two generations, a complete change of caste status may be achieved.

CONCLUSION

The role of bilateral kinship in caste affiliation—the fact that ritual rank descends through both men and women—has already been stressed. If *all* kinship connexions—except those which have been repudiated by excommunication—are relevant in assessing ritual status, then the only way of marking the complete separation and distinction of a 'caste status' group is to preserve all marriages within an endogamous circle.

Complete endogamy is the most effective method of preserving status. A second way—if the status-bearing groups are not entirely endogamous—is the use of hereditary names and pedigrees. For this reason, although kinship is bilateral, the aristocrats in Kandyan villages often claimed to possess patrilineal pedigrees which justified their titles and ranks. Such named 'patrilineal houses' were not exogamous lineages.

A third way to distinguish status groups in a bilateral kinship system is by locality. And here Gālpitiya is a good example. A fourth is by occupation. The role of caste occupations is obvious in this respect.

All these four methods are used in the Kandyan hills to perpetuate and to safeguard ritual purity, or to demonstrate claims regarding status, with varying degrees of emphasis.

CASTE PRINCIPLES IN A KANDYAN COMMUNITY

We have been concerned with the flexibility of caste principles in the spheres of endogamy and ritual status. In doing so, I have drawn attention to irregularities of practice which contrast with what Professor Lévi-Strauss has called 'the conscious model' of social structure (1953: 526), the core principles of caste distinction. These irregularities are significant, for the resolution of contradiction itself demonstrates the power of caste concepts.

I have shown (a) how cross-caste unions did not affect caste boundaries which were re-established in every case; (b) how changes in ritual status were 'validated' by recourse to traditional 'identification marks' which reaffirmed the values inherent in them.

It does not seem to me likely, then, that there will be any early abandonment of caste principles, even under conditions of improved physical mobility and urbanization. [14]

NOTES

[1] In these respects, as in his garments, the Buddhist monk imitates the behaviour of a Hindu *sannyasi* (cf. Carstairs 1957: 101–2; Coplestone 1892: 456–7; Zimmer 1946: 162 n.).

[2] One *pāla* of land is the area sown with one *pāla* basket of rice seed. It is a variable area of round about half an acre.

[3] (This is not the universal opinion. Elsewhere in Ceylon a Goyigama villager remarked 'There must always be caste, for at festivals we need drummers and if there were no Tom-tom Beaters who would do the drumming?' E.R.L. Ed.)

[4] A typical *vasagama* would be, for example, Senanayaka Seneviratne Herat *Mudiyansē* lā gē Welakona Watte *Gedara* Banda: that is, Banda of the House (*Gedara*) of Welakonawatte descended from Knight (*Mudiānse*) S. S. Herat (see Pieris 1956: 172; Tambiah 1958: 24).

[5] In the Maritime Provinces the status of the Karāva is very high. They claim Kshatriya descent. In the interior, where the Goyigama predominate, they are not accorded the same respect.

[6] This use of *gē* needs to be clearly distinguished from the Low Country Sinhalese '*Gē* name' to which Ryan (1953) refers rather frequently.

[7] The normal word for wife is simply 'woman' (*gǟni*); *pavula* is more polite, and the politest is 'lady' (*hāmine*).

[8] Expressed in the phrases—*yanni enni ne*; *kanni bonni ne*; *sambanda ne* (lit. no going and coming; no eating and drinking; no marriage). More directly, they may say, *näkam kädīla* (kinship is broken).

[9] In all cases known to me the husband is rich and the girl's parents benefit from the association. They may even receive some money, but such pseudo-bridewealth payments are always kept secret, for it would be said that the woman has been 'prostituted' for material gain.

[10] These are in the Nuwara Eliya Kachcheri. I was allowed access to them by the kind permission of Mr B. F. Perera, C.C.S., then Permanent Secretary to the Ministry of Home Affairs.

[11] In the Registers of 1857–61 eight aristocratic houses own, between them, 196 *pāla* of paddy; twenty-one ordinary Goyigama families own 188·5 *pāla*; those of low rank own only 35 *pāla*. Le Mesurier (1898: 266 ff.) provides both land and population figures. He gives an average land holding for 'Terutenne' as a whole,

excluding Gālpitiya but *including* all low castes, as 0·534 *pāla* per head. For Gālpitiya alone the average is 0·15 *pāla* per head.

[12] Share-cropping (*andē*) arrangements in Terutenne were as follows: the cost of buffaloes and seed was shared, and the harvest was divided fifty-fifty between tenant and landlord.

[13] Dehi Gaha Pitiya Kalu Banda is a 'low' Goyigama name comparable to Galpitiya Banda (p. 107); Nissanka Mudiansēlāgē Tun Amunu Gedara is a 'good' Goyigama name containing *vasagama* and *gedara nāma*. (See p. 106 and note 4 above.)

[14] The fieldwork on which the essay is based was supported by a Fellowship from the Wenner-Gren Foundation and an Anthony Wilkin Studentship from the University of Cambridge. I should like to express my most sincere thanks to both these bodies as well as to the Master and Fellows of Peterhouse for electing me to a Bye-Fellowship to pursue my researches.

THE SYSTEM OF
SOCIAL STRATIFICATION IN SWAT,
NORTH PAKISTAN

By FREDRIK BARTH

INTRODUCTION

The present paper describes the system of social stratification in the Swat area of North Pakistan. It is a hierarchical system of stable social groups, differing greatly in wealth, privilege, power, and the respect accorded to them by others. The local term for such groups is *qoum*. In any such system the organization of one stratum can only meaningfully be described with reference to its relations to the other strata, and in the pages which follow the various *qoum* are analysed as parts of a single, larger system embracing the whole community, and not as autonomous social units. My concern is with social structure, not with ritual or religion, and, for my purpose, although the people of Swat, as Sunni Moslems, fall far outside the Hindu fold, their system of social stratification may meaningfully be compared to that of Hindu caste systems.

Caste, as a pattern of social stratification, is characterized by the simplicity of its basic schema, and its comprehensiveness. In contrast, class systems (in the sense used by Warner 1942) give simultaneous recognition to a multiplicity of conflicting hierarchical criteria, while systems of rank, though single in the scale which each defines, are generally restricted in their fields of relevance.

The simultaneous comprehensiveness and clear definition of units which characterizes caste systems results from the summation of many part-statuses into standardized clusters, or social persons, each identified with a specific caste position. Thus, in a Hindu caste system, there is a diversity of economic statuses and ritual statuses, but these are interconnected so that all Priests are sacred and all Leatherworkers are untouchable.

A sociological analysis of such a system naturally concentrates on the principles governing the summation of statuses, and the consequent structural features of the clusters of connected statuses or caste positions. Every individual has statuses in the occupational framework of the community, in the framework of kinship relations, etc. The caste system defines clusters of such statuses, and one particular cluster is imposed on all individual members of each particular caste.

The coherence of the system depends upon the compatibility of such associated statuses. The members of the society itself justify the clusters by asserting an inherent compatibility in a moral or ultimate sense. Thus, among Hindus, the concept of pollution serves to define which statuses should be combined, and which are incompatible. In Swat, other concepts, such as privilege and shame, serve similarly as explicit justifications. But sociological principles are also involved in the question of compatibility. Each caste position must be such that the requirements implied by its component statuses may be simultaneously satisfied; and the alignment of each individual in terms of his different statuses should also be consistent and not fraught with interminable dilemmas. The former aspect of compatibility relates to roles, the latter to the degree of congruence between different organizational frameworks. In the essay which follows both aspects will be explored.

The area under discussion constitutes the main section of a large, fertile valley, roughly seventy by thirty miles, in tribal territory in the northern part of West Pakistan.[1] A major part of the valley lies within the borders of Swat State, a small part in Dir State, and the remaining, lower part, in Malakand Agency—all recent political subdivisions of minor significance to the present problem.[2] The climate is fairly dry, but water for irrigation is plentiful. In the valley bottom, the population depends on cereal agriculture, particularly of rice, for its subsistence. This valley area has a population density of roughly 1000 per square mile, and is extensively irrigated by the Swat river and its main tributaries. Settlement is in compact villages numbering from 100 to 5000 houses (each occupied by an elementary family). The mountainous areas bordering on the valley have a much sparser population, scattered in hamlets of five to twenty houses. In these hill settlements, maize is the main cereal, but pastoral pursuits are important as well.

The total population of the whole Swat Region is about half a million, dependent throughout on a complex subsistence economy. Agricultural techniques are sophisticated, and include crop rotation, the use of decomposed natural fertilizer, etc. Craft specialization is also highly developed. In contrast, communications are poor. Each community is largely self-sufficient and all are of similar type, though varying in size. Politically, the area is anarchic. The self-sufficient communities do not depend on wider co-ordinating agencies of any kind, and internally there is much conflict and factionalism. Swat communities have never been subject to external government. Such centralized institutions as exist are weak and are a recent internal development. All major political decisions, the conduct of law, and the protection of life and property are the responsibility of members of the local community, whose actions are governed mainly by internal considerations.

Each Swat community contains a number of unequal groups, known as *qoum* (sing.) in the Pokhto (Pashtu) dialect of Swat. The general meaning of this term is 'tribe, sect, people, nation, family' (Raverty 1867), but in Swat it is used predominantly as a term for these hierarchically-ordered social groups, though occasionally also for religion or sect. A full list of such groups will be given below; in a general way they fall into the following categories, in descending rank order: (1) persons of holy descent, (2) landowners and administrators, (3) priests, (4) craftsmen, (5) agricultural tenants and labourers, (6) herders, and (7) despised groups. All these groups are represented in nearly every village; in varying degrees each is dependent on the skills and services of all the others, and together they form the community.

The various *qoum* are not strictly homologous—the kinds of criteria which define membership, and the internal organization of each group, differ quite profoundly. Furthermore, there is no ritual system in terms of which the groups are compared and ordered with respect to each other. In contrast to a Hindu caste system there is no symbolic framework within which the homology of the groups may be expressed. Social stratification is expressed in everyday profane situations in a vast number of different ways, but never as a single, comprehensive system. Moreover, the Muslim religion, to which the whole population subscribes, explicitly repudiates the very social differences which the existence of *qoum* implies. Sacred activities continually assert the basic unity and equality of all Muslims.

Swat *qoum* are thus not castes in the Hindu sense of the word; yet they are too diverse and rigidly separate to be described simply as social classes. Furthermore, Swat lies on the edge of the Indian world and partakes to a certain extent in Indian traditions. Thus the different *qoum* within a single community participate in non-monetary reciprocal services on the model of the Hindu *jajmani* system, and the relative ranking of many occupations, and even their names, correspond to those of the villages in the Indian plains, and so on. For the rest of this paper I shall in fact refer to the Swat *qoum* as castes. It must be remembered that they are castes only in a very general sense. Taking Hindu caste as the ideal type, the Swat variety is a limiting case.

HISTORICAL SUMMARY

Something needs to be said here concerning the historical background of contemporary Swat society. History explains the presence of Indian cultural influences and illustrates the ethnic multiplicity of the 'castes' which make up the communities of modern Swat. In addition, history is used by the people of Swat themselves to explain the relative social standing of different castes.

Though Swat lies in the middle of a turbulent cultural shatter zone, it is geographically isolated in that no major routes of communication pass through the valley. Within the last century neighbours within a radius of 100 miles have variously paid taxes to Peking, Bokhara, Kabul, and Delhi, but Swąt has probably never paid tax to any external government. Yet it has had contact with all the major political currents in the area, and the first historical mention of the valley goes back to a hymn of the Rigveda (Stein 1929: viii). Very dense populations were established at an early date, as is shown by Greek (327 B.C.) and Chinese (A.D. 519) records. After a Buddhist phase Hindu religion reasserted itself, so that, at the time of the Muslim invasions (A.D. 1000) the population was solidly Hindu (*ibid.* ix). These invasions caused no break in local traditions: in the place-names given in the early Greek sources may be recognized the names of the major villages of modern Swat (*ibid.* 47, 60). Conversion to Islam was thus something imposed by a small group of warrior lords, with the bulk of the population maintaining its secular Indian traditions. The main body of the modern agricultural tenants in Swat, who are without known ancestry, probably descend from this formerly Hindu population. Some basic modern village institutions may reasonably be assumed to represent continuations of ancient Indian originals.

The first Muslim masters of Swat were non-Pathan Dilazak tribes from South-East Afghanistan. These were later ousted by Swati Pathans, who were in turn succeeded in the sixteenth century by Yusufzai Pathans. Both groups of Pathans came from the Kabul valley. The Yusufzai form the present caste of landowners. Some groups of agricultural tenants trace Dilazak and Swati descent, while a group of Swatis whose ancestors were displaced by the Yusufzai invasion form the landowners along the east bank of the Indus. The present political and economic dominance of the Yusufzai landowners is justified by the people themselves by reference to this history of conquest.

The diversity of castes in Swat has also been augmented by infiltration. Since the time of the conversion to Islam, a number of local lineages claiming descent from the Prophet Mohammed, or from prominent Saints, have swelled the ranks of the Saintly caste. These migrant 'saints' came mostly from Turkistan. Rival 'saint' groups from Persia, representing the Shiah schism, have been unsuccessful in the exclusively Sunni Swat. From lowland India, Gujar pastoralists speaking the Gujri language have moved up into the area and appropriated the occupation of herders. These same people have also established themselves as a dependent tribe of nomads and hill cultivators. Other small tribelets of unknown origin are today assimilated to the Gujar caste by virtue of their pastoralist way of life. Certain occupational castes are alleged to be recent immigrants from the lowlands, a view supported by their physical characteristics. Thus the caste of muleteers which monopolizes trade and transport is supposed to be of Bengali origin; these people are said to have arrived in Swat about 200 years ago. Similarly the leatherworkers are thought to be recent immigrants from Panjab. Barbers regard themselves as the local representatives of a homogeneous barber caste found throughout

Pakistan and Northern India. Finally, with the growing sophistication of Pathan chiefs, a need has arisen for the services of sweepers. During the past thirty years about a dozen families of Sweeper caste have been brought into the valley from the Pakistan plains.

This historical sketch highlights the capacity of the Swat *qoum* system to accommodate diverse ethnic groups within a framework of discrete categories, and the intimate connexion of this system with the traditions of India. But unlike the Hindu caste system, the basic organizational framework is defined, not by ritual, but by occupation and division of labour. I shall therefore first describe the positions of the castes of Swat with regard to occupation and then proceed to discuss other types of relationships.

OCCUPATIONAL FRAMEWORK

A complete list of all the caste groups to be found in the Swat area would have to be based on very extensive census surveys, for many groups are small and found in a few localities only. The following list, based on censuses of six villages in different parts of the area, includes all groups of any numerical importance. They are:

	Occupational category	Pashtu name
1.	Descendants of the Prophet	Sayyid
2.	Saints of various degrees, all landowners and mediators in conflict	Sahibzada Mian Akhundzada Pirzada
3.	Landowners and warriors	Pakhtun
4.	Priest	Mullah
5.	Shopkeeper	Dukandar
6.	Muleteer	Paracha
7.	Farmer, tenant	Zamidar
8.	Goldsmith	Zərger
9.	Tailor	Sarkhamar
10.	Carpenter	Tarkarn
11.	Blacksmith	Inger
12.	Potter	Kulal
13.	Oil-presser	Tili
14.	Cotton-carder	Landap
15.	Weaver	Jola
16.	Leatherworker	Mochi
17.	Agricultural labourer	Dehqan
18.	Herdsman	Gujar
19.	Ferryman	Jalawan
20.	Musician and dancer	Dəm
21.	Washerman	Dobi
22.	Barber	Nai
23.	Thong- and sieve-maker, dancer	Kashkol

These are the alternative names by which persons will identify themselves when asked what is their *qoum* (caste).

Let us first regard this simply as a system of occupational statuses, a scheme for the division of labour. These occupational statuses are rigidly segregated and cannot be combined, except in the following cases: a priest, as well as being in charge of a mosque, is expected to support himself by agriculture (as proprietor of dedicated lands or as a tenant) and by trade; carpentry may be combined with blacksmithing, as a basis for specializing in the construction of watermills; and herdsmen may engage in agriculture, as tenants or labourers. But it is impossible to work simultaneously as an oil-presser and as a tenant, as a tailor and as a shopkeeper, as a leatherworker and as a thong- and sieve-maker. Even personal versatility is unusual; it is regarded as quite inappropriate for a tenant to mend his own plough. On the other hand the products or services of specialists in each of these twenty-two occupations are all equally essential. All the occupations must therefore be represented in each self-sufficient community.

Pathans, however, distinguish quite clearly between caste status (*qoum*) and occupational status (*kasb, kar*); it is quite possible for a man to say: 'I am a Carpenter, but I am working as a muleteer.' This does not mean that he is at one and the same time both carpenter and muleteer; it means that his caste status is 'Carpenter', but his occupational status is 'muleteer'. Despite this the occupational system provides the basic conceptual framework for the interrelations of castes. Caste status is ascribed to individuals by virtue of their paternity, while occupations are the subject of individual choice. But 'being of Carpenter caste' means, in Swat, that you are *expected* to work as a carpenter; any other occupation, though formally open, is regarded as anomalous. Caste status and occupational status are not identical, but each caste position is identified with an occupational position. As well as being the ideal, this identification corresponds very closely to empirical facts: of the 476 heads of households registered in the complete censuses of four small villages, only 16 % were engaged in occupations inappropriate to their caste. The correlation of caste status and occupational status in one of these villages is shown diagrammatically in Fig. 2.

The significance of this discrepancy between caste and occupation will be discussed in the second part of this essay but, for the moment, I shall ignore it. First, I shall describe the productive system of Swat, and show how this is relevant to (a) the rigid segregation of statuses in the occupational system, (b) the effects which each occupational position has on the position and organization of the caste occupying it, and (c) the composition of local communities which results from these factors.

The distinguishing feature of the productive system of Swat is that, although it depends on a high degree of individual specialization and division of labour, it functions with a very small volume of exchange medium in an essentially non-monetary economy. The rigid segregation of occupational statuses follows directly from these facts. Because the volume of money is small it is difficult to provide for the extensive exchange of services and goods. What is exchanged is *services*, rather than either money or goods. There is a complex pattern of reciprocal services within groups of persons who have direct social relations with one another. To make such a system of exchange function, the respective services due from each participating member must be clearly defined, and kept rigidly separate. The Swat 'caste' system may thus be seen as a device whereby a high degree of occupational specialization may be achieved in a non-monetary economy.

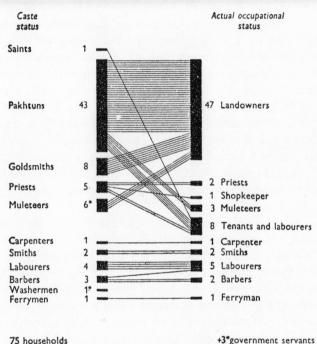

Fig. 2. Castes and occupations in Worejo.

The main products of the Swat valley are agricultural and a predominant fraction of the population is engaged, directly or indirectly, in agricultural activity. Agricultural production is maintained by pooling the resources and labour of a number of specialists, including as a minimum: landowner, tenant and/or labourer, carpenter, smith, muleteer, and rope- and thong-maker. Each of these contributes to the total production in the following manner:

(1) By and large only members of the Pakhtun or Saintly castes own land and among these most land is concentrated in the hands of a small number of prominent chiefs and landlords who do not themselves engage in manual

* Two men of Muleteer caste and one of Washerman caste worked as government servants and were outside the occupational hierarchy.

labour. Their contribution to the productive team is to provide the land. Sometimes they also supply seed and equipment.

(2) The agricultural work itself—ploughing, seeding, irrigating, harvesting, etc.—is done by tenants and agricultural labourers. Their tools and equipment —yokes, ploughs, harrows, etc.—are wrought by the carpenter and the smith, who also perform all repairs on these implements.

(3) Transport—of seed, fertilizer and crop—is provided by the muleteer.

(4) Ropes, brooms, sieves, pitchforks tied with thongs, bridles for the mules, etc. are made and repaired by the rope- and thong-maker.

In a monetary economy, the co-ordination of such various specialists could be achieved through a system of wages or cash payments between dyads, such as employer/employee, buyer/seller, etc. But the people of Swat, though long familiar with money, have no centralized institutions to which they would grant the authority to mint coins, and they have not developed any convenient alternative exchange media. Grain is extensively used in payment for contractual services of long duration, but grain is too bulky to be readily transferred. Substantial quantities of money (now predominantly in the form of Pakistan Rupees) reach Swat from the outside through government subsidies, exports and migrant labour. But the volume of this exchange medium is not nearly sufficient to serve the internal exchange requirements of a diversified population of half a million people.

The co-ordination of these occupational specialists must thus be achieved in an essentially non-monetary economy. This is done through the formation of productive teams, in many ways analogous to the European medieval manor. Within such teams each specialist contributes with the skills and equipment or resources appropriate to his status, and receives in return a fraction of the resultant product. The members of each team are in constant communication with one another, and co-ordinate their activities in a manner analogous to what industrial sociologists call 'continuous flow production'. Thus the tool-makers do not produce ploughs, ropes, etc. autonomously, to store in a shop and have on hand in case of future need; instead they work in response to the specific requirements of the tenants in their team, who in turn accommodate their pattern of work in the fields to the workshop and transport facilities provided in their team. The members of the team thus form a single co-ordinated productive unit, with communications passing directly from every member to every other member.

In the definition of its boundaries, and in its system of sharing profits, each team is hierarchically and centrally organized. The landowner is the pivot on which the organization is based. The team is formed through a series of dyadic contracts between the landlord and each separate specialist; there are no contracts between the different specialists, although in fact they directly co-ordinate their work. Similarly, remuneration for services flows from the landlord and not from the persons to whom the actual services were rendered. Thus, a blacksmith produces a plough on the request of a labourer, because they belong in the same productive team, both having contractual relations with the same landowner. The labourer gives the smith no remuneration for this service. At the completion of the productive cycle, both smith and labourer receive their reward in the form of a share in the joint production of the team—a certain number of tons of rice and wheat. They receive this from the landowner, who himself took no part in the reciprocal system of services, but with whom all the contracts were established.

This pattern of organization, and the flow of remuneration, may be expressed diagrammatically as in Fig. 3.

The duties implied by each status position in the system are traditionally defined, the share of each in the total product likewise. The carpenter contracts to produce and maintain all implements or parts of implements traditionally made by carpenters which are necessary to maintain production—that is, all wooden equipment used by tenants, labourers, smiths, and muleteers at any time working on the estate. No record is kept of the actual jobs done by each person—they do what needs doing, for a contractual minimum period of one agricultural season. At the completion of the harvest and threshing, the tenant or labourer call all his team partners to the cleaned and dried grain piled beside the threshing-grounds among the fields. In the simplest case, shares in the crop are then allotted, under the supervision of the landowner, to all who are members of the productive team, and to each in proportion to his traditional claim.

The crop is laid out in long rows of small, equal piles. The landlord himself, or his estate overseer, then passes along the rows and allots one in every four to the tenant (or one in every five to the labourer, that is a man who has contributed labour only, not, as the tenant, with seed and bullocks as well), one in every twenty to the muleteer, one in every forty to the carpenter, one in every forty to the smith, and occasional piles as alms to the poor. The rope-and thong-maker usually receives a set amount yearly. In this way, every member of the team receives his fraction of the gross product, while the remainder—in fact a lion's share—goes to the landowner.

Variations from this most common procedure all follow the same general pattern. Sometimes one productive team works the land of several landowners; but in such cases, although the work in the different fields is coordinated, the landlords themselves do not pool their resources. The product of each field is divided separately.

The historical connexion of this pattern of organization with the Hindu *ajmani* system is obvious. More important in the present context is its effect on the occupational status system. The organization of work depends on a clear delimitation and allotment of duties to each member of the group, while the pattern of remuneration similarly requires adherence to a traditional schema for the allocation of duties and rights. The system breaks down if any individual assumes duties which are proper to status positions other than his

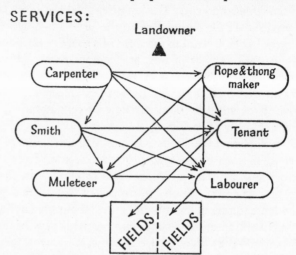

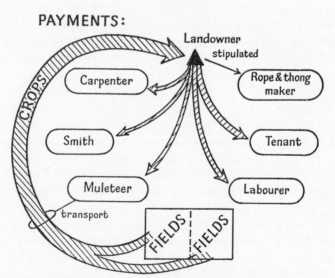

Fig. 3. The organization of agricultural activities in Swat: services and remuneration.

own. The smith who services an estate will claim his contractual share of the produce even if a tenant has done some of the smith's work; and there is no way to adjust the division of the produce so that both parties will accept the adjustment as a fair settlement.

If the occupational contracts are to retain their functional simplicity, they must cover the complete roles of the traditional statuses. The remuneration goes to the holder of a role; it is not a reward for 'piecework'. And these roles are furthermore so balanced in relation to the yearly cycle of labour requirements that it is very difficult for an individual to combine two roles at once. For example, in the peak season of agricultural activity, at the times of harvests and rice transplantation, there are brief periods when, under the traditional system, all the available labour both agricultural and non-agricultural is in full employment at the same time. A man who was at once both a tenant and a smith would be unable to carry out his seasonal smith duties because he would already be fully committed to agricultural duties in his capacity as tenant. The system thus requires a strict segregation of the different occupational roles. This segregation is achieved, in Swat, by the close identification of occupational status with caste status.

The other specialists in the community are mostly the parties to similar contracts. Priests serve local sections of communities which have the form of territorially delimited wards or parts of wards. In return the priest obtains the use of dedicated land and certain kinds of yearly tax, in kind. Most landowners have a potter, a tailor, a herder, and a washerman attached to their households on a yearly contract, whereby each is expected to perform all services appropriate to his caste in return for a stipulated weight of grain per year. Apart from such dyadic contractual relations the services of such professional craftsmen are also available to others on a piecework basis. This is true too of the other, rarer, specialists not discussed so far. These sporadic and limited 'piecework' exchanges require money payment and haggling over prices. The only case where goods are paid for in kind as opposed to money is in exchanges between agriculturalists and herders, where the traditional equation of equal volumes of milk for maize holds good.

There is one further field of non-monetary exchange which should be mentioned. This concerns the status position of barbers and the exchange of the goods and services required for the *rites de passage* of every individual. Villagers in Swat mark the birth, circumcision (for boys), betrothal, marriage and death of individuals by fairly large-scale public celebrations. For the purpose of mutual assistance in performing these celebrations they form neighbourhood associations, *taltole*. Each such association is administered by a barber; he holds service contracts with each individual household in the association, whereby he agrees to perform the service appropriate to his caste in return for a stipulated yearly payment and traditional gifts. These services include haircutting (of men by the barber, of women by his wife) and shaving, but they also include the organization of celebrations, the announcement of the event to appropriate outsiders, and the mobilization of the assistance from fellow association members to which each family is entitled. This assistance includes contributions of foodstuffs and cooked foods, firewood and crockery, and help in cooking and serving. The 'low', 'taboo' status of the barber stems from this special role. Because it involves intimate contact with the domestic life of each family, in breach of the usual barriers of prudery and seclusion, the barber's status needs to be clearly segregated from that of other persons in the community.

CORPORATE ORGANIZATION AND SPATIAL DISTRIBUTION OF CASTES

While caste is closely identified with occupation, the relation between caste and political organization is more remote. The political organization of the villages of Swat depends on a system of balanced opposition between landowners competing within a feudal framework. Politically, the whole region is insecure and anarchic, and individuals seek security by attaching themselves to powerful chiefs. Such attachments are contractual, and are immediately linked with the individual's house tenancy. A landowner automatically gains administrative authority over the individuals residing on his property; in return, he is responsible for protecting their lives and interests.

The administration of each community is in the hands of public assemblies of landowners. A landowner will act as advocate for all his non-landowning tenants. After a legal decision has been reached in this forum, it is left to the aggrieved party to compensate himself at the expense of his opponents. It is therefore important for every non-landowner to have a powerful landowner as political patron. A good patron is one whose word carries weight in the assembly, and who will thereafter be able to extract restitution on behalf of his political clients.

But the landowner in turn depends for his position on the fact that he controls many followers. Every landlord therefore endeavours to reinforce his authority by binding his followers with additional economic obligations. By making gifts to the occupants of his 'men's house' he seeks to obtain their exclusive allegiance. In awarding house tenancy contracts he tries to restrict the allocation to those who are willing to make other kinds of dependency contract with him at the same time. In the simplest case, the productive teams described above emerge as corporate political groups under the leadership of the landlord. In all cases, the economic bonds of dependence between persons of differentiated status are utilized to increase the authority of the political lord. Through this organization, the community is split up into homologous sections under rival leaders on the basis mainly of house tenancy contracts. Each such section forms a political group which contains within it a number of different mutually dependent statuses having the landowner as common political patron of all.

Such an organization is entirely independent of caste; it further prevents the castes themselves from developing corporate administrative functions in any system like that of the local and regional caste panchayats of India. In Swat, no form of organization which cuts across the attachment of the clients to their patrons would be tolerated. Thus, with some minor exceptions, which we shall discuss below, the castes of Swat do not form corporate groups. Indeed, it is hardly possible that they should. The productive system which I have described has the necessary implication that the membership of each of the inferior dependent castes is widely dispersed and consists of small pockets of population located in the feudal domains of a large number of

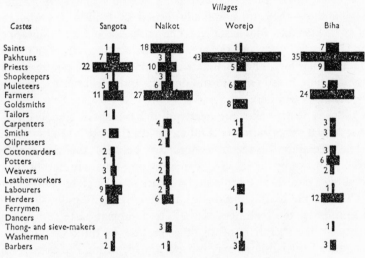

Fig. 4. The caste composition of four Swat villages.

different land-owning chieftains. The membership of such a dispersed group has no common interest or estate in terms of which it might be 'corporate'.

In different local communities the proportions of each caste vary. Fig. 4 shows the caste composition of four particular small villages. The main differences are of two kinds: (a) There is variation in the ratio of Saints to Pakhtuns—some communities are dominated by the former, but most by the latter. (b) There is an inverse variation in the ratio of landowners to tenants. The ratio of total agriculturalists (owners plus labourers):to total craftsmen:to total service castes is roughly constant, though adjusted to the differing labour requirements of different areas. The constancy of these ratios seems to be maintained by migration in response to a free labour market— for it must be remembered that all economic relations are based on voluntary individual contracts; there is no serfdom. Some specialized castes are found in a few communities only. Ferrymen are distributed only among the communities on the banks of the Swat river, butchers are found only in major towns. Where they occur such specialists constitute only a small minority of the population.

To this pattern of distribution there are certain exceptions. In the hilly and mountainous areas of Swat are many small hamlets which do not participate fully in Pathan economic and social life. They are inhabited in part by Gujar pastoralists and farmers ethnically distinct from Pathans, and in part by remnant lineage segments of former landowning groups who were driven off their estates in the main valley during past conflicts. In the feudal framework of Swat, these hamlets correspond to the *coloni* settlements of the Roman marches—they are nominally owned by landowners who reside in the valley bottom and who exact irregular corvée labour and military service; but the land is too poor and the area too difficult to control for the landlord to extract regular tax. These hamlets maintain their own political authorities and organization, based on caste and descent, and fall in most respects outside the system discussed here.

The villages of the valley are nearly all multi-caste in composition, and in these the feudal organization is combined with the caste system in a different way. The necessary degree of congruence between the two structures is secured by ascribing feudal ascendancy in any one community to a single high-ranking caste. True corporate structure is then given to this one caste only. This is done by making one caste the sovereign landowners. Thus, in each community, the members of the one dominant caste serve as political patrons to all the members of all other castes. In these circumstances the feudal rights of the landlord may be interpreted, within the caste framework, as merely one further set of rights pertaining to high-caste position. We find that, depending on their relative positions of dominance as landowners, either Pakhtuns or Saints may assume these feudal privileges. In any one community all the individual feudal patrons, being of a single caste, are equal in rank but are ranged in opposition against the feudal patrons of rival neighbouring communities, especially if these are of another caste. In this case the political boundary between territorial ('feudal') domains coincides with the caste boundary between Saint and Pakhtun, so that the political ideology and the caste ideology serve to reinforce each other.

The members of a dominant caste must sometimes join in corporate action for purposes of government and the defence of their privileges. The land tenure system involves the periodic re-allotment of fields to title-holders over a considerable area, and this presupposes a corporate organization of landowners (Barth 1957). Although they differ in power according to the number of their clients, all landowners are equal in rank, and the institution which provides a corporate expression of the local dominant caste is simply a plenary assembly of all its members; this assembly simultaneously constitutes the governing body of the whole local community.

The caste unity of the landlord group is not easily maintained. Land is held as individual, private property and can be bought and sold. Since feudal powers go with land, the structure calls for some legal device which will (a) prevent lower-caste individuals acquiring both land and feudal powers, and (b) eliminate those members of the dominant caste who have lost their land and feudal powers.

The former requirement is satisfied by restrictions on the individual's right to alienate land, and by distinguishing between different kinds of title to land. First, close agnates, neighbours and the headman of the ward (administrative division of the village) have first option, in that order, to buy any land offered for sale. Secondly, the transfer of complete title is not permitted across caste boundaries. The vast majority of land is owned by Pakhtuns, who trace descent from patrilineal ancestors who are supposed to have acquired holdings by conquest during the sixteenth century. Such land is classified as *daftar* and the title-holder has full rights of sovereignty. *Daftar* title gives the holder the right to speak in the assembly. *Daftar* land sold to another Pakhtun remains *daftar*, and the new owner succeeds to the complete rights. If however it is alienated to an individual of another caste, whether Saint or lower caste, it is classified as *siri* land. The buyer of such land obtains full rights to the land as private, disposable property; but its conversion to *siri* has divorced it from the administrative framework of the feudal system and removed the right of its owner to speak in the assembly. The exclusive right of members of the Pakhtun caste to serve as patrons is thus maintained in spite of the alienation of full economic rights over part of the original Pakhtun land. A tenant resident on *siri* lands cannot be the political client of his landlord; he must find some other patron, either through land tenancy contracts with a *daftar*-owning Pakhtun or by establishing other ties of obligation and service.

Conversely, the Pakhtun who loses all his land loses his caste status. Since his claim to Pakhtun status can no longer be validated by the possession of *daftar*, his right to speak in the assembly of landowners is lost, and he must become the client of another man. In spite of his descent, he is then sloughed off from the higher caste and assimilated into the caste of farmer-tenants.

An essentially similar system is enforced in the villages ruled by Saints— the right to speak in the assembly, and thus to serve as political patron to others, depends on the ownership of land plus membership in the Saint caste.

It should be noted that, while the caste unity of local landowners is essential in both cases, unity of descent is not required. Patrons of different grades of Sainthood, with different ancestors, sometimes rule together within a single village, while, occasionally, villages dominated by Pakhtuns contain non-Yusurzai as well as Yusufzai lineage segments. [3]

The development of trade and the increase in money circulation have lately introduced special factors which are influencing the pattern of caste distribution, and hence the degree to which particular castes are 'corporate'. Most money income in Swat comes from the sources I have mentioned. This money is used to buy a great variety of foreign trade goods. These include foodstuffs such as refined sugar and tea, and industrial products such as crockery, factory-made rifles, cloth, and medicines.

Under the more anarchic political conditions which formerly prevailed, trade caravans required military protection. Each chief provided the defence equipment for the caravans run by his own dependent muleteers. In this way trade remained under the control of the feudal leaders. However, with the improved communications and greater security which developed about the turn of the century, trade became more regular, and trading bazaars grew up in the main communication centres. This bazaar trade has remained predominantly in the hands of former muleteers, now liberated from their dependence on military protectors. Such groups of muleteer traders now tend to congregate in the trading centres.

Within the limits imposed by the shortage of exchange media this same type of trade is also used for internal exchanges between the different local communities. This makes it possible for fellow specialists who are not directly involved in agricultural labour to congregate in a village by themselves where they can maintain themselves by exporting their specialized products to neighbouring villages and buying the necessities of life from outside. This arrangement is particularly feasible for weavers. Throughout the Swat valley there are to be found occasional villages inhabited almost exclusively by weavers; these form centres for the production of cloth.

Here, then, two kinds of localized caste groups have developed: (a) groups of traders located in communication centres who are independent of agriculture but possess money resources, and (b) small villages of uniform caste serving as centres of specialized production for a monetary market. Both types of localized caste group tend to develop a corporate structure. This takes the form of a ritual association (taltole), the general nature of which has already been explained above (p. 123) in connexion with the role of barber. In both cases independent action by the localized castes is opposed by the landowners, but the castes are able to maintain the autonomy because of their freedom from dependence on feudal patronage. As individuals the traders are mostly house-tenants of various landowners, but they are able to repudiate their individual obligations of clientage in favour of the organized support of their own local caste group. Traders organized in local groups can be useful to the feudal leaders as providers of capital. Also, the possession of money allows such people to protect their interests with occasional bribes. Weavers, on the other hand, generally congregate on the land of a single, non-resident owner; and being economically independent they can combine to keep the landlord's influence at a minimum, in much the same way as do the Gujar hamlets mentioned above (p. 126).

The communities of traders and weavers both tend to recognize, informally, as local leader and spokesman, a *masher* ('elder' or senior man), but in both cases the web of community relations evoked through joint participation in the feasts of *taltole rites de passage* provides the main mechanism for co-ordinating common caste action. New arrivals, such as traders transferring their business from another village, or weavers settling in a new community, are not expected or compelled to join their fellow caste members in any formal organization. There is no 'guild' and no coercion to accept the authority of a *masher*. Only when the newcomer has established a set of informal or formal social ties with his fellow caste members, and started to participate in their association for *rites de passage*, is he expected to show solidarity with the group and to participate in their efforts at corporate action.

The Pathan combination of feudal and caste organization thus depends on the maintenance, in the ruling groups only, of an approximate identity between feudal and caste lines of cleavage. Where economic statuses based on trade and a monetary economy are established outside the feudal framework, other inferior castes also tend to develop corporate organizations. It is remarkable that, in this strongly Muslim area, these latter incipient corporate organizations do not take the form of guilds; instead they appear as ceremonial commensal units concerned with the celebration of the *rites de passage* of caste members.

KINSHIP AND CASTE

Caste, in this essay, is analysed not as a set of ritual groups, but as a pattern of social stratification—that is, a conceptual scheme for ordering the individuals of a community, each occupying multiple statuses, in terms of a limited set of hierarchical categories. Caste systems are considered to be characterized by the relatively high degree of congruence that obtains between (*a*) the various status frameworks found in the community, with their internal hierarchies, and (*b*) the hierarchy of caste categories. This congruence is achieved by the definition of invariant and imperative constellations of statuses.

In these terms, we first described the set of caste categories in Swat, and showed the close congruence between this system and the occupational framework. Then we analysed the nature of the congruence between the political framework and caste. As a result, certain constellations of statuses became apparent: Pakhtuns are high rank, landowners, and political patrons; persons of Smith caste are lower rank, blacksmiths, and political clients, etc.

We have now to analyse the nature of the congruence between the caste categories and the mutual attachment of individuals through ties of kinship. This congruence is produced in all caste systems by making an aspect of kinship the primary vehicle for the transmission of caste positions; by the ascription of caste on the basis of parentage. Where children are ascribed to the caste of their parents and castes are endogamous, all ties of kinship become concentrated within castes, and the lines of kinship cleavage coincide with the boundaries between castes.

Such perfect congruence will be disturbed wherever there is 'social mobility'. There is in fact a considerable amount of such mobility in Swat; but this in part serves to preserve, rather than disturb, the characteristic constellations of statuses defined in the caste hierarchy. The kinds of social mobility of relevance to this material fall under three headings: (1) true individual mobility, whereby a man changes his caste position during adult life; (2) hypergamy and hypogamy, whereby a woman marries into a caste different from her own; and (3) intergenerational mobility, whereby a child fails to be ascribed the caste position of his parents.

Whereas cases of (1) seem to be very rare in Swat, (2) and (3) are fairly frequent. All three processes deserve explanation and discussion.

1. *Individual caste mobility*

There is an oft-cited popular saying in the Peshāwar district, to the effect that 'last year I was a Julaha (Weaver); this year I am a Shekh (Disciple); next year if prices rise I shall be a Saiyad' (Ibbetson 1916: 222). This points to what is undeniably the easiest route for individual caste mobility—that leading to Sainthood. In Peshāwar City such mobility implies little more than a change in honorific title, but in Swat the transition involves change of caste, and is much harder to achieve.

The theological basis for the occasional recognition of Sainthood among non-Saints is a folk elaboration of certain Koranic suggestions regarding incarnations. Pathans believe that in every generation a certain number of very sacred persons (such as a *Ghous*, a member of the committee ruling the Heavens) are born among us, to live a pious life without disclosing their identity. Recognizing and paying respect to such persons gives religious merit.

The man who leads a pious life thus receives particular respect; he cannot make any explicit claims to Saintly status, but may in time be granted such status by others. Usually recognition does not come till after his death, and final proof of his sanctity derives from the efficacy of his grave, evaluated in a spirit of empiricism. For example, the sanctity of a minor Saint in one of the areas where I worked was discovered accidentally from the power of his grave. A shepherd boy let his goats graze between the graves; one nanny-goat disrespectfully leapt over this man's grave so that her teat brushed against it. Her udder immediately became inflamed, and the goat died shortly. The villagers realized there was power in the grave; when put further to the test it proved a potent shrine for prayers for the fertility of stock and women. The deceased man was then recognized as a Saint, and his descendants are now treated as members of the Saint caste.

But recognition may also come in the Saint's lifetime, as in the case of the Akhund of Swat, the prominent religious leader of the last century, who was originally of Tenant caste. A change of residence and a long period of seclusion seem to be invariably required in order to effect such a transition from a lower-caste status to the caste status of Saint.

The following is a summary of the career of the Akhund of Swat. Born west of the Swat river, he first supported himself as a herder; he then moved to the bank of the Indus and there retired to the life of an ascetic for twelve years, attracting pilgrims and disciples, but taking no part in secular life. In the course of this period he was recognized as a Saint. On his return to secular life he made extensive use of the special peace-making privileges of his acquired caste status so as to further his political career. After his period as a recluse he married and had sons, and his descendants are now classified as *Mians* (cf. p. 117). It should be noted that he did not return to his community of origin or re-establish contacts with collateral kin there.

This pattern of *rite de passage* can be duplicated in the careers of many less important 'created' Saints. During their period of ascetic seclusion they are referred to as *Pir*; only when they re-emerge in secular life are they reclassified as belonging to the grade of Sainthood, a position which affects the status of their descendants within the caste.

No other institutionalized pattern of caste mobility is known. Pakhtun caste status depends on descent and land ownership, both of which are unobtainable by outsiders because of the process whereby alienated land is reclassified as *siri* (see above, p. 127). Mobility between different low castes can be achieved by deception only, as when a person who has competence in the occupation of a caste other than his own travels to a distant place where he then pretends to be of that caste. Similarly, loss of caste cannot take place within a man's own lifetime. A man who was born a Pakhtun will remain a Pakhtun, even if he later loses his land, since he can maintain his claim on the pretext that alienation of land was enforced, or temporary. But such a man has no *daftar* and thus no Pakhtun status to pass on to his sons. Downward mobility thus results from a failure of succession, not from a change in the individual's own adult caste position.

The rules relating to individual social mobility thus serve to maintain the congruence between the framework of discrete castes on the one hand and the web of kinship affiliation on the other. They do this in two ways. Firstly, the possibility for individual upward mobility is blocked. In the one case where such mobility is possible, the mobile individual (would-be Saint) is required to dissociate himself entirely from his original kin, and the separation of his old and his new status is further marked by an extended intervening period of seclusion and non-participation in secular life in either capacity. Secondly, the possibility of individual downward mobility is blocked by holding over the completion of the process until the next generation.

2. *Hypergamy and hypogamy*

The principle of caste endogamy is usually discussed in terms of Hindu concepts of pollution rather than with reference to its structural significance; and in the former framework one is easily driven to purely scholastic explanations of the widespread phenomenon of hypergamy (e.g. Stevenson 1954: 57). In the present discussion both hypergamy and hypogamy will be treated as special forms of social mobility which have a direct relevance to the degree of congruence which obtains between caste and kinship. Obviously, any marriage across caste lines creates kinship ties between individuals in different castes and such links persist into succeeding generations. A pattern of caste endogamy has the structural effect of preventing the development of such cross-caste kin relationships. In Swat, however, the ban on individual caste mobility for males is not reinforced by any effective check on this form of mobility for females. Although there is a clear tendency towards caste endogamy, the contrary cases are very numerous (40%; see Table 5, p. 135).

The importance of separating kinship relationship from intercaste relationship stems from the importance of kinship in the transmission and ascription of statuses and rights. This does not imply that all social relations between castes need to be repudiated. Intimate individual ties across caste lines form an inherent part of any caste system, and are implied in the obvious complementarity of different caste roles. Strong affectual ties between members of different castes are perfectly compatible with the smooth functioning of a caste system. Only those intercaste relations which would create ambiguity in the principles of status ascription are incompatible with the structural features of a caste system. It follows logically from this that a pattern of caste endogamy is vital in any system of kinship only where rights and status are transmitted to children from *both* their parents. But in the Pathan case the system of patriarchal family structure and exclusively patrilineal descent serves to make matrilineal and matrilateral kinship irrelevant to status and authority ascription, and thus obviates the need for caste endogamy. To demonstrate this fully would require considerable documentation of the ethnographic facts relating to Swat Pathan kinship and marriage, some of which can only be sketched here. The main factors to be considered are the form of marriage, descent, and the distribution of authority between kinsmen.

Pathans recognize only one form of marriage; it is made legal by a simple Islamic ceremony; and by this ceremony, and this alone, the husband obtains full and exclusive rights over the wife. Brideprice payments, often of considerable magnitude, may be necessary to make the father or marriage guardian give his legally required consent to the marriage; but their payment or non-payment in no way affects the nature or extent of the husband's rights over his wife. On marriage, all the legal rights formerly held by the father, as well as exclusive sexual access, are vested in the husband. A married woman cannot administer her own property, she may not enter any contract except with the permission of the husband, the husband has the right to demand obedience, and the right to discipline his wife to secure such obedience. For the protection of her own, limited, rights, the wife turns not to her father, but to the village headman or *Qazi*. This corresponds very closely to the Hanafi legal code.

Naturally, even though legal ties are severed, a woman's affectual ties with her parents and siblings normally persist after marriage; however, a wife must obtain her husband's permission before visiting her parents, and he has the full right to refuse her such permission and cut her off from all communication with her kin. On the death of her husband a woman's own son becomes her marriage guardian; only if she has no male issue do potestal rights revert to her father or brother. Affines, if they are friendly with each other, participate extensively in each other's associations for *rites de passage*; but when disagreements arise such participation is temporarily or permanently discontinued. There are no occasions when co-operation or even communication between affines is mandatory. This description of the authority relations within a household and of the relations between affines displays a family system which one might characterize as 'strongly patriarchal'. This pattern of authority must be distinguished from the pattern of descent, which relates to the transmission of statuses and not to the distribution of authority. While in the former case our attention centres on affines, in the latter we are concerned with distinctions between patrilateral and matrilateral relatives. Pathans combine a patriarchal family system with exclusive recognition of patrilineal descent. The greater part of the rights and obligations which define the position of a Pathan in his various spheres of activity are the subject of private contractual agreements, but all those formal positions to which there is hereditary succession are transmitted exclusively in the male line. Membership in a descent group (*khel*) is transmitted from father to son; there is no pattern of matrilateral grafting, and adoption is impossible. Chiefship in feudal states passes, in default of direct male descendants, to agnatic collaterals of the deceased chief, never to a sister's son or daughter's son, and the status of the mother—whether of chiefly birth or low birth—is immaterial. Seniority among brothers, sons of a common father, is determined by relative age, without reference to the seniority of wives, their respective mothers. Virtually all property, movable and immovable, is held by men and inherited patrilineally, without regard for Islamic laws of inheritance. Women may receive gifts and thus have possessions, or the husband may endow his wife on marriage with a special amount of property (*mahr*), but except for items of personal use such property is held by the husband on the wife's behalf and inherited by her sons. These personal possessions of a woman are inherited by Islamic law, sons each taking two shares and daughters each one share. Where a woman has such property of her own, it is transferred to her marital home upon marriage. She retains no rights in her natal home and therefore has no such rights to transmit to her children. There are thus no material interests of any kind which bind persons to their matrilateral relatives. Pathans usually have affectual ties with their mother's brothers and maternal grandparents, but such feelings have developed simply as a result of childhood visiting—subject to the father's control. Senior matrilateral relatives are shown the respect due to them by virtue of their sex and age, neither more nor less.

In sum, marriage alters the affective significance of kinship for the woman herself, but affinal relations do not create ties between households, and matrilateral kinship plays no role in the transmission of status of property, or in the distribution of authority of seniors over juniors. All status and property is held and transmitted by the male line, and all familial authority is exercised by male patrilineal relatives.

This pattern of descent and authority by itself ensures the necessary degree of structural congruence between significant kinship alignments and lines of caste cleavage: caste ascription, like all other hereditary ascription of status, is on the basis of patrilineal descent; the kinship ties of individuals, both with respect to rights and obligations and in terms of authority relations, are similarly defined on the basis of patrilineal descent alone.

The figures listed in Table 5 show a marked tendency towards caste endogamy, but this endogamy does not arise from any need for a precise congruence between the alignment of individuals by kinship and by caste. In the Pathan system, endogamy seems rather to relate to the hierarchical aspects of caste and to the denial of identity between castes. Pathans explicitly state that sister exchange can only take place between equals. It is appropriate for people who are alike and is a good thing as an expression of solidarity. Any kind of kin endogamy, or status endogamy, is thus approved as an overt expression of friendliness, and as a factor creating friendliness by virtue of the intervisiting which is expected to follow. But women may also be given unilaterally to unequals.

As in most of western Asia and India, women are regarded as an appropriate form of tribute from the weak man, who seeks protection, to the strong, who gives it. The value of such hypergamous marriages to the wife-givers springs, not so much from the value of the affinal relation thus established, as from the esteem acquired through giving highly valued 'tribute'. Hypergamous marriages are thus a recognized pattern; in contrast, hypogamy—the giving of a woman downwards, to inferiors—is frowned upon and considered a 'shame' for the woman's family. Claims to relative rank between castes are usually made in precisely such terms—Saints say they receive wives from Pakhtuns, but will not give them daughters in return.

Table 5. *The caste status of living spouses in four villages*

Figures from villages of Sangota, Worejo, Nalkot, Biha.

MAN	WOMAN Saint	Pakhtun	Priest	Goldsmith	Muleteer Shopkeeper	Farmer	Craftsman	Labourer	Herder	'Unclean'
Saint	25	17	4	0	0	0	0	0	0	0
Pakhtun	6	90	5	3	7	3	4	5	1	0
Priest	8	11	29	0	0	5	3	1	4	1
Goldsmith	2	1	0	9	4	0	0	0	0	0
Muleteer Shopkeeper }	0	2	1	1	16	3	4	1	0	1
Farmer	0	6	7	0	4	42	8	0	10	1
Craftsman	0	2	1	0	4	9	29	2	6	1
Labourer	0	0	0	0	0	3	4	13	6	0
Herder	0	0	0	0	0	2	1	0	17	0
'Unclean'	0	0	2	0	1	2	0	2	1	14

Total marriages 476

Marriages endogamous to caste 283 = 60%
Hypergamous marriages   110 = 23%
Hypogamous marriages   83 = 17%

One final factor helps to obscure the effect of this explicit rule, namely the adjustable brideprice. Most of the cases of apparently hypogamous marriages which appear in Table 5 might, if the matter were argued properly during the marriage negotiation, be represented as marriages between near equals; any reluctance on the bride's family could then be overcome by a higher brideprice offer. Thus, in seventeen of the nineteen cases of marriage between a man of Priest caste and a woman of Pakhtun or Saint caste, the man belonged to a colony of land (*siri*) owning Priests who are established in the village of Sangota. Such men are lower in caste status than their Pakhtun fathers-in-law, yet, for purposes of argument, they can be classified as 'fellow land-owners'. Generally speaking, brideprice varies in terms of two criteria which are made quite explicit during brideprice negotiations.

(1) Where husband and wife are of approximately equal status then the higher the status of the husband the higher the brideprice.

(2a) Where the situation is one of hypergamy the brideprice due under (1) is cancelled.

(2b) Where the situation is one of hypogamy the brideprice due under (1) is increased.

The net result of such manœuvres is that, as shown in Table 5, a substantial proportion of all marriages are cross-caste. Even so the tendency towards caste endogamy is quite explicit. Each caste is commonly regarded as constituting the widest order of kin group (*nasab*), that is to say it is thought of as endogamous.

3. *Intergenerational caste mobility*

In Swat society the rules of marriage do not, as in an orthodox Hindu system, automatically establish a congruence between the frontiers of caste and the frontiers of kin grouping, but, even so, the principle whereby caste membership is inherited by patrilineal descent does require that individual descent groups should be confined to particular castes. Although this congruence of descent grouping and caste grouping is in fact maintained, a certain amount of intergenerational caste mobility does occur.

Pathans themselves are fully aware of such caste changes, and relate the process to occupational mobility. Thus, if the son of a Priest takes up carpentry, he will always be known as a Priest, likewise his son again. But if a man of the third generation continues as a carpenter and there are no known collateral agnates in other occupations in the village, people may say: 'his father was a carpenter, and so was his grandfather; so he is a Carpenter (by caste).' Such a process is entirely consistent with the facts described above: the reclassification is done without reference to matrilateral kin, and is made possible by (a) stability of occupation in the descent line, and (b) absence of collateral agnates in other occupations. The founder of this new 'lineage' of Carpenters—the deceased ancestor who changed his occupation—may well be remembered as having been a Priest, so long as no other agnatic descendants of his are known. Under these particular circumstances, intergenerational mobility (and retroactive reclassification of immediate ancestors) preserves rather than disturbs the characteristic constellation of statuses defined by each caste. A patrilineal descent group such as this is unconnected with other such groups, it occupies the socio-economic position characteristic of carpenters, and thus clearly belongs in the caste category 'Carpenter'.

The depth and span of patrilineal descent groups varies between castes, and to some extent within them. While Saints recognize numerous quite distinct lineages, some large, some small, Pakhtuns in theory, and very nearly in practice, make up a single very large patrilineage. Among Farmers and

Herders some ramifying descent groups of six to eight generations' depth are found; these occasionally have an additional pedigree which links them to distant tribes of past conquerors. Carpenters, Potters, and particularly Black-smiths, though possessing only very shallow genealogies nevertheless have a distinctive pattern of genealogical claims. An important section of these craftsmen claim descent from King David, who, in the manner of a culture hero, forged tools, using his knee as an anvil, and with these tools made a potter's wheel—thereby inventing the techniques of smithing, carpentry, and pottery-making. He taught these arts to his sons and daughter; the latter was taught pottery, but she then married and communicated her skills to her husband and son. All 'true' craftsmen claim descent through one of these siblings from King David, and occasionally claim that this is what makes them distinct from mere *kasbgər*—craft-companions. However, only about one-third of the Smiths in Swat seem to claim the distinction of descent from David, and the tradition is without much importance as far as members of other castes are concerned.

The process whereby, as a consequence of change of occupation by an ancestor, a whole patrilineage may 'change its caste' is relevant for the forma-tion of new castes. The framework of occupations itself is not entirely stable—for while no traditional occupations are known to have disappeared, some new ones are definitely known to have arisen. New castes may form around such new occupations through hereditary transmission from father to son; alternatively a new caste may be formed through the splitting of an old one. Both processes may be seen at work today. The introduction of the sewing-machine some seventy years ago has led to the emergence of a new, as yet small and not fully formed, caste of 'Tailors', recruited from a variety of castes in the middle range of the hierarchy. Similarly, the invention, outside of Swat, of a form of sandal which in the course of the last thirty years has become the predominant fashion in men's shoes, has created the new occupa-tion of 'sandal-maker'. A variety of men have adopted this occupation, and my Pathan informants expected that a caste of 'Sandal-makers' would emerge in the course of another generation or two. On the other hand, over the last sixty years improved communications have led to a wide proliferation of shops. Formerly, all such shops were owned by Hindus; but recently there has developed a local Pathan caste of 'Shopkeepers'. Though it has received accretions, particularly from the Priest caste, the main body of this new caste derives from the traditional Muleteer caste, with which it is still sometimes identified. It is a reasonable presumption to expect that within a generation or so 'Shopkeepers' and 'Muleteers' will emerge as completely distinct castes.

To sum up: congruence between the boundaries of caste grouping and the boundaries of kinship obligation is maintained by confining each patrilineal descent group to a particular caste. Where social mobility occurs across caste boundaries various kinds of fission of the patrilineage may result which serve to restructure the kinship system into segregated caste compartments as before. The exclusively patrilineal emphasis among Swat Pathans implies that hereditary succession and the jural allocation of authority in terms of kinship is confined within particular patrilineages. This suffices to ensure consistency between caste roles and kinship roles. The self-sufficiency of the

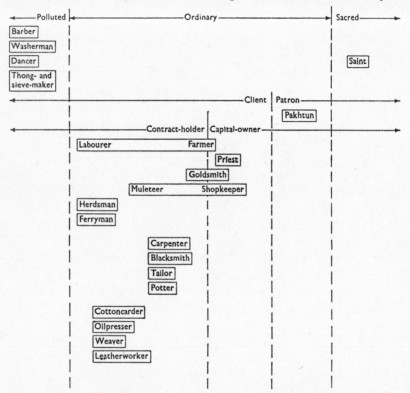

Fig. 5. The hierarchy of castes in Swat, and some criteria on which it is based.

patrilineal principle accounts for the relaxation of the ordinary caste rule of endogamy. The existence of affinal links which cross caste boundaries has no consequences as regards jural authority over things or persons.

HIERARCHICAL ASPECTS OF CASTE

The main clusters of statuses that characterize each caste position in Swat should now be clear, as well as the types of relation—economic, political, and matrilateral—which exist between castes. But a caste system does not only serve to place individuals in discrete categories; like any system of social stratification it also provides for a hierarchical ordering of these categories into 'higher' and 'lower'. This hierarchical ordering may be referred to as the *ranking* of castes. The rank order of castes is made explicit in various ceremonial contexts; it may also be elicited by direct questioning of informants. The positions of the castes in the high–low axis in fig. 5 summarizes, to the best of my understanding, the numerous explicit and implicit statements I collected on the subject.

These evaluations are made on the basis of such criteria as wealth, skin colour, political power, belief in inherited virtue, etc. In the present section I attempt to isolate these criteria. I must stress that among my informants no single individual was ever willing to produce an exhaustive schema for the ranking of all castes. The problem is thus one of analysis and synthesis.

A distinction may usefully be made between the *criteria* for the ranking of groups, and the *idiom* in which hierarchy is expressed. In a Hindu caste system, it would appear that a single concept underlies both criteria and idiom—namely the concept of ritual pollution. But in Swat the position is less simple. The *ranking* of castes derives from a whole set of value scales, of which purity/pollution is only one—political power, and wealth, being others. The *idioms* in which these ranking differences are expressed are on the other hand highly eclectic, and consist mainly of a series of actions expressive of equality or inequality between persons. I shall first discuss the criteria by which the hierarchical ranking of castes in Swat seem to be determined, and secondly the idioms in which hierarchical differences are expressed.

CRITERION OF PURITY/POLLUTION

In contrast to Hinduism, Islam is an egalitarian religion; and an elaborate hierarchy of ritual rank has no meaning in an Islamic framework. This is not to say that there is no development of a concept of pollution; but, according to Islam, ritual pollution, which derives from body processes such as elimination, sexual intercourse and death, applies equally to all. All men are equally cursed with such sources of pollution, and purity can only be maintained by repeated purificatory acts on the part of the individual. As a ritual system Islam is thus unsuited to produce hierarchical distinctions between social strata. However, this ideal ritual equality does not imply that Moslem societies are without ritually based systems of social stratification.

In Swat, as in Hindu societies, the notion that pollution derives from body processes marks off certain castes as occupationally polluted. In the case of Sweepers this pollution is so strong that the profession as such has been rejected by Pathan society. The only Sweepers to be found in Swat are members of a Panjabi caste who have been brought in and protected by prominent chiefs. The indigenous polluted castes include Washermen, Barbers (who are concerned with shaving, nail-paring, and childbirth), and Thong- and Sieve-makers (who work with the guts of animals); these three groups are everywhere despised and form the lowest stratum of society. The caste of Dancers also falls in this category, since they are associated with prostitution and other morally bad practices.

These polluted castes constitute only a small percentage of the total population (cf. Fig. 4). There is no agreed principle whereby other occupations may be rated as more or less polluting, consequently the majority of the population remains, in this respect, undifferentiated and is of 'normal ritual status'. The concept of pollution produces no further distinctions until we reach the very top of the hierarchy, where a belief in the inherited power and holiness of the descendants of the Prophet Mohammed, or of prominent Saints, serves to set these persons apart from ordinary profane individuals. Such elevated status, however, here requires more strict observance of ritual rules, and not the abandon characteristic of Indian Sanyasis.

The criterion of purity/pollution thus gives a tripartite ranking of castes in the categories (1) *polluted*, embracing the four lowest castes, (2) *ordinary*, representing the bulk of the castes, and (3) *sacred*, represented by the highest caste, the Saints.

CRITERION OF POLITICAL POWER

Political power is highly valued among Pathans; it is associated with independence and regarded as honourable and good, whereas weakness and dependence is shameful and bad. The important distinction for purposes of ranking is between *patrons* and *clients*; patrons include all Pakhtuns and Saints, clients all others. However, since Pakhtuns are politically more powerful than Saints, this introduces some ambivalence in their ranking vis-à-vis Saints, an ambivalence not unfamiliar elsewhere in India.

Politically powerful Pakhtuns can denigrate the sacred status of Saints and claim rank equality with them; Saints on the other hand are adamant in their claim that all Saints *ipso facto* rank higher than all Pakhtuns. On this issue the Saints have the support of the non-Pakhtun population.

As noted above (p. 124), the political authority of patrons over their clients depends to a considerable extent on economic control. The criterion of political power thus produces a further distinction: between (*a*) castes whose members are economically free, and (*b*) castes whose members depend on their political patrons for economic contracts. The politically more autonomous castes include the Priests, who farm or administer dedicated lands, some Farmers, who themselves own a bit of land, Goldsmiths, who have their own capital and engage on piecework only, and Shopkeepers, who do independent business on a cash or barter basis. Economic contract-holders, on the other hand, whether tenants, labourers or craftsmen, are subject to economic sanctions from their patrons. They are weaker and more dependent, and thus rank lower.

CRITERION OF WEALTH

Ranking on the basis of wealth differences tends throughout to be congruent with the ranking on the basis of pollution and political power, with two exceptions. Dancers may accumulate a fair amount of wealth, particularly in the form of pretty clothes, even though they belong in the lowest, polluted, group; on the other hand Saints cannot compete with Pakhtuns in wealth even though they claim the highest 'ritual' status. In both these cases, the criterion of purity/pollution dominates over that of wealth, so far as general ranking evaluations are concerned.

In all other respects the criterion of wealth serves to reinforce the ranking based on other criteria. In some cases it serves to intensify the differentiation between castes. Thus Labourers, Herdsmen, and Ferrymen are all economically depressed castes, and as such they rank lower than the other craft and service castes, even though they stand higher than all the polluted groups.

The relative hierarchical positions of the castes of Swat are thus consistent with, and seem to derive from, the three widely held value criteria of purity/pollution, political power, and wealth. Each of these criteria produces one or several dichotomies, placing groups of castes in positions of inequality. In combination, these three criteria produce all the apparent rank distinctions except one, namely that between high- and low-status craftsmen: that is to say between (a) Carpenter, Smith, Tailor and Potter, who are high, and (b) Cotton-carder, Oil-presser, Weaver and Leatherworker, who are low. This distinction is quite clearly recognized by Swat Pathans. Whereas carpentry, smithing, etc. are regarded as perfectly respectable occupations, weaving, oil-pressing, etc. are not respectable, and the castes associated with these latter occupations may be referred to by others as 'low' and 'unclean'. The nature of the value criterion on which this ranking is based is obscure. A similar ranking is found in North India, where it is said to be justified in terms of the Hindu pollution concept (Stevenson 1954: 61, but see comment by Mayer 1956: 128 n.). Such arguments appear to be meaningless in terms of the ideas of Swat Pathans, but we may be dealing here with a direct case of cultural diffusion from India. The castes of Swat correspond to, and their members communicate with, those of the North Indian plain; and general 'snob' attitudes current in India may have been adopted in Swat without reference to the philosophic values underlying them. In all other respects, however, the ranking of castes in Swat may be seen to reflect basic values which are prevalent in Swat itself.

HIERARCHICAL COMPATIBILITY OF PART-STATUSES

I have shown above how the caste system of Swat is characterized by the principle of status clustering—groups of compatible part-statuses are associated together and thus form a single stereotyped social person characteristic for each caste. The members of the caste are then made to conform to this stereotype. As pointed out above (p. 114), this matter has two aspects:

(1) Compatible statuses must imply roles that may be simultaneously satisfied by one individual.

(2) In a structural sense compatible statuses must define positions that are congruent with one another. While in most of this essay I have emphasized the former aspect, I am here concerned with the latter. I seek to discover possible structural principles that govern the association of statuses in clusters.

Clearly we are concerned with rank. To be compatible, part-statuses must imply similar relative positions in the general scale of superordination/subordination. Thus a man cannot simultaneously be an economic contract-holder and a political patron, since in one capacity he would rank low while in the other capacity he would rank high and be expected to exercise authority over his (economic) superiors. While such incongruities are possible in a society where the different offices and capacities of a single individual are distinguished, they are disruptive to a system where these are *not* clearly distinguished, and where individuals have intimate, face-to-face relations with each other in many different spheres of activity. Differentiation in such societies can only be maintained if individuals in their different capacities are ranked consistently. This is precisely what is achieved in a caste system by limiting the permitted combinations of part-statuses to a restricted number of constellations.

Pathans in Swat express the notion of compatibility and incompatibility of statuses in terms of a concept of shame (*sharm*). A man is 'ashamed' to assume any position or perform any action which he feels is incompatible with his caste status. Considerations of shame and its avoidance are very frequent and prominent in conversations and deliberations in Swat. In fact the concept applies in a number of different situations; it is brought into play whenever an individual's actions deviate from the norm of what is expected of him, it thus also relates to activities such as hospitality, blood feud, etc. In its relevance to caste, shame expresses precisely the notion of hierarchical incompatibility of statuses and roles, and applies equally to up- and down-grading: for example, a Carpenter refuses, from shame, to perform a polluting service like washing clothes for another, while feelings of shame similarly prevent him from trying to exercise authority over a caste superior, such as a Pakhtun or a Saint who is in debt to him. The use of this shame concept by Pathans corresponds to the use of the pollution concept among Hindus.

Shame directs the choices made by individuals in assuming new part-statuses. The caste organization depends for its maintenance on the explicit recognition of this discriminating factor.

HIERARCHICAL IDIOMS

In Swat hierarchical differences are continually being expressed in ceremonial behaviour; but the idioms in which they are expressed are not developed into any coherent system like that of Hindu ritual. Such idioms mostly concern the relative status of pairs of actors, rather than of whole caste groups. A brief description of these idioms will help to give a fuller picture of the social implications of caste in Swat.

Economic prosperity correlates highly with caste rank, and since affluence is readily visible in dress, the style of clothing (quality, number and size of garments, cleanness, weapons carried, etc.) is used as a rough sign of caste. Only Saints, however, stand out clearly by their use of white cloth, particularly in the use of white turbans.

Saints are also marked off as a category by special deference behaviour: when any member of the Saint caste enters a room, all those present rise— a sign of respect which is also shown to prominent chiefs as individuals, but not to any other whole caste group. Hierarchy is also constantly expressed in terms of address. The kinship terms *Baba* (GrFa), *Kaka* (FaBr), *Wrora* (Br) and *Haleka* (Boy/Son) are often used vocatively in a metaphorical sense, the choice of term reflecting relative status rather than age. Thus all adult males of the Saint caste are addressed as *Baba* by all others, while persons of low caste extend this term also to senior Pakhtuns and Priests. An adolescent Pakhtun, on the other hand, freely uses the term *Haleka* to older men of lower caste: for example, to craftsmen. But the most important hierarchical idioms derive from the two fundamental situations of gift-giving and commensality.

We have here to distinguish between gifts = charity, and gifts = tribute. Some kinds of goods are used in both contexts, and an observer needs to have previous knowledge of the relative statuses of the two actors to understand the meaning in each case. Thus a gift of fruits is an appropriate sign of deference, but also, inversely, it is a sign of benevolence. Other goods may be used only, or primarily, in one context. Thus gifts of money are frequently made, but only *from* a superior *to* an inferior; they are often described by the Arabic (Muslim) word for alms. Snuff, on the other hand (used by most adult males), is offered only to equals and superiors, and not to persons of inferior status.

Large feasts with multi-caste participation—which occur very frequently in Pathan men's houses—are the most characteristic setting for the expression of rank. Cooked food may appropriately be given not only to equals but also to inferiors. Hence, if a person of superior rank eats the cooked food of an inferior, he honours the latter by implying a rough equality between the two. This relates to the fact that the giving of food, particularly in the form of a meal, implies an obligation on the part of the host to protect his guest in a political sense. The host is the (political) superior of the guest. The superiority is temporary in the case of a visitor, but of indefinite duration when the recipient is a local person. Crucial political ties between allies, and between leaders and followers, are thus expressed in the joint participation in a feast.

In contrast, actual commensality, at close quarters, implies an approximate equality of rank. A feast can thus provide opportunity for the expression of a fairly complex set of relative differences and equalities. Feasting usually takes the following form: political unity, which cuts across caste boundaries, is asserted overall, but with an authority differentiation marking the host as leader and the guests as allies and dependants. The guests divide into three degrees—high-rank, commoner, and low-rank individuals; these group themselves in concentric circles, with the persons of high rank in the centre. Meals are generally served on trays each with a feeding capacity of four to eight. Several individuals of equal status seat themselves around one tray. Alternatively the three degrees of rank may be served with food in succession. Saints and Priests are sometimes isolated in one corner of the men's house and fed separately. Women never participate in such feasts; even in the home, the two sexes eat separately, particularly among the higher castes.

CONCLUSION

As has now been shown, the system of social stratification in Swat is a system of clearly delimited, named positions, into one or another of which all members of the community fall. The series of such positions is hierarchically ordered, and is differentiated with respect to functions and relative access to coveted goods. Each position is characterized by a cluster of statuses relevant in different sectors of life and frameworks of organization. Thus, for example, a *Pakhtun* is a *wealthy* man of the *Yusufzai descent group*, a *landowner* and a *political patron*, while a *Smith* is a man of *moderate* means, a putative *descendant of David*, *blacksmith* by profession, and a *political client*.

In other words, despite the highly complex system of differentiated statuses and division of labour within the society all members may be placed in one or another of a limited set of positions. This is possible because the incumbency of one status also necessarily implies incumbency of a series of other statuses forming the cluster characterizing that 'caste position'. By Nadel's definition, the system is highly *involute*, though this term was developed by him mainly to characterize homogeneous societies (Nadel 1957: 67-72).

THE SYSTEM OF SOCIAL STRATIFICATION IN SWAT

The principle of status summation seems to be the structural feature which most clearly characterizes caste as a system of social stratification. It is mainly for this reason that I have referred to the system of hierarchical positions in Swat as a caste system. I am aware that I thereby give the word a wider application than may suit many students of Indian caste systems. However, if the concept of caste is to be useful in sociological analysis, its definition must be based on structural criteria, and not on particular features of the Hindu philosophical scheme. In this sociologically more fundamental sense, the concept of caste may be useful in the analysis of non-Indian societies.

In much of the Middle East, 'plural' societies are found, characterized by clear lines of internal segmentation, often based on ethnic criteria; such societies have a structure characterized by the summation of statuses in an involute system, in which a high degree of status differentiation is associated with a limited set of permitted status combinations. Such systems depend for their persistence on very clear criteria for status ascription. In societies other than those of extreme patriliny, this prerequisite implies a pattern of endogamy within the stratified groups—a feature often emphasized in the definition of caste. An analysis of such societies along the lines suggested here might make it possible to isolate other such prerequisites or correlates of caste.

The necessity for status summation in standardized clusters or positions, and the rigid differentiation of such positions in Swat, has been shown to be functionally related to the requirements of an elaborate system of division of labour in an essentially non-monetary economy (cf. p. 118). I would put forward the following general typology under which the features discussed here might be subsumed:

There are (1) truly homogeneous societies, in which internal differentiation is weak. Almost unlimited social substitution is possible within sex and/or age categories. Increasing status differentiation impairs this substitutability unless (2) clusters of statuses are defined. In that case the possibility of substitution remains, but only within a limited set of hierarchical categories ('castes') which are interdependent and together compose the community. Considerable complexity is possible in such a system without the development of any bureaucratic form of organization.

Finally there are (3) complex systems in which different statuses can be freely combined. Here the different capacities of the different statuses are clearly distinguished. This type of system is found associated with the use of a monetary medium which facilitates the division of labour.

Caste systems belong to the second category; but in my view this category is not confined to the classical caste systems of Pan-Indian civilization.

FREDRIK BARTH

NOTES

[1] The author did fieldwork in the Swat valley during nine months of 1954. Other aspects of the material have been discussed in Barth 1956 and Barth 1957.

[2] The Malakand Agency was established by a British military expedition in 1895. The territories held by Dir were conquered by that state in the first years of this century. Swat State was founded in 1917 and recognized by British India in 1927. The changes in social organization wrought by the weak and unstable centralized governments of Dir and Swat have so far been limited, while the villages of Malakand Agency have complete local autonomy.

[3] No account is taken here of possible consequences of Pakistani plans to create elected bodies based on universal suffrage. Any such organization, if successful, would clearly prove fatal to the structure I have described.

BIBLIOGRAPHY

BADEN-POWELL, B. H. (1892), *Land Systems of British India*, vol. III, Oxford.
—— (1896), *The Indian Village Community*, London.
BAILEY, F. G. (1957), *Caste and the Economic Frontier*, Manchester.
BANKS, M. Y. (1957), 'The Social Organisation of the Jaffna Tamils'; unpublished Ph.D. thesis in Cambridge University Library.
BARTH, F. (1956), 'Ecologic relationship of ethnic groups in Swat, North Pakistan', *American Anthropologist*, vol. 58, no. 6.
—— (1957), 'The Political Organisation of Swat Pathans'; unpublished Ph.D. thesis in Cambridge University Library.
CARSTAIRS, G. M. (1957), *The Twice Born*, London.
CARTMAN, J. (1957), *Hinduism in Ceylon*, Colombo.
COHN, B. S. (1955), 'The Changing Status of a Depressed Caste', in *Village India* (ed. Marriott), Chicago.
COPLESTONE, R. S. (1892), *Buddhism*, London.
COX, O. C. (1948), *Caste, Class and Race*, New York.
DAVIS, K. (1951), *The Population of India and Pakistan*, Princeton.
D'OYLY, SIR JOHN (1929), *A Sketch of the Constitution of the Kandyan Kingdom*, Colombo.
DUBE, S. C. (1955), *Indian Village*, Ithaca.
DUMONT, L. (1957a), *Une Sous-Caste de l'Inde du Sud: Organisation Sociale et Religion des Pramalai Kallar*, Paris.
—— (1957b), 'Hierarchy and Marriage Alliance in South Indian Kinship', in *Occasional Papers of the Royal Anthropological Institute*, no. 12.
—— (1957c), 'For a Sociology of India', in *Contributions to Indian Sociology*, No. 1 (ed. Dumont and Pocock), The Hague.
FORAL, –. (1920), *Of the Kingdom of Jafnapatam and the Vany* (original version 1645 translated and edited by P. E. Pieris), London.
GERTH, H. H., and MILLS, C. W. (1947), *From Max Weber: Essays in Sociology*, London.
GOUGH, E. K. (1955a), 'The Social Structure of a Tanjore Village', in *India's Villages* (ed. Srinivas), Bengal.
—— (1955b), 'The Social Structure of a Tanjore Village', in *Village India* (ed. Marriott), Chicago.
—— (1955c), 'Female Initiation Rites on the Malabar Coast', in *Journal of the Royal Anthropological Institute*, vol. 85, pp. 45–78.
—— (1956), 'Brahman Kinship in a Tamil Village', in *American Anthropologist*, vol. LVIII, no. 5, pp. 826–53.
HEMINGWAY, F. R. (1906), *Madras District Gazetteers: Tanjore*, Madras.
HOCART, A. M. (1931), *The Temple of the Tooth in Kandy*, London.
—— (1950), *Caste: a Comparative Study*, London.
HUTTON, J. H. (1946), *Caste in India*, Cambridge.
IBBETSON, SIR DENZIL (1916), *Punjab Castes*, Lahore.
IYER, K. R. SUBRAMANIA (1928), *The Mahratta Rajas of Tanjore*, Madras.
K.M.D.A. (1952), *Kandyan Marriage and Divorce Act, No. 44 of 1952*, Colombo.
KNOX, R. (1911), *An Historical Relation of Ceylon*, Glasgow.
KROEBER, A. L. (1931), 'Caste', article in *Encyclopaedia of the Social Sciences*, London.
LEACH, E. R. (1955), 'Polyandry, Inheritance, and the Definition of Marriage', in *Man*, vol. 55, art. 199, London.

BIBLIOGRAPHY

LE MESURIER, O. J. R. (1898), *Handbook of the Nuwara Eliya District*, Colombo.

LÉVI-STRAUSS, C. (1953), 'Social Structure', in *Anthropology Today*, Chicago.

LEWIS, O. (1958), *Village Life in Northern India*, Urbana, Illinois.

LEWIS, O., and BARNOUW, V. (1956), 'Caste and the Jajmani System in a North Indian Village', in *Scientific Monthly*, vol. 83, no. 2.

MAJUMDAR, R. C., RAYCHAUDHURI, H. C., and DATTA, K. (1946), *An Advanced History of India*, London.

MAYER, ADRIAN C. (1956), 'Some Hierarchical Aspects of Caste', in *Southwestern Journal of Anthropology*, vol. 12, no. 2.

NADEL, S. F. (1957), *The Theory of Social Structure*, London.

PETER OF GREECE, PRINCE (1955), 'Polyandry and the Kinship Group', in *Man*, vol. 55, art. 198, London.

PIERIS, R. (1956), *Sinhalese Social Organisation*, Colombo.

POCOCK, D. (1957), 'The Bases of Faction in Gujerat', in *The British Journal of Sociology*, vol. VIII.

PRABHAVANANDRA, S., and ISHERWOOD, C. (1947), *Bhagavad-Gita*, London.

RADCLIFFE-BROWN, A. R. (1939), *Taboo* (the Frazer Lecture for 1939), Cambridge.

RAGHAVAN, M. D. (1951), 'Ethnological Survey of Ceylon, No. 2—The Kinnarayā—the Tribe of Mat Weavers', in *Spolia Zeylanica*, vol. 26, part II.

—— 'Ethnological Survey of Ceylon, No. 4—The Ahikuntakayā—The Ceylon Gipsy Tribe', in *Spolia Zeylanica*, vol. 27, part I.

RAVERTY, H. G. (1867), *A Dictionary of the Pukhto*, London.

REDFIELD, R., and SINGER, M., eds. (1955), *Comparative Studies of Cultures and Civilizations: Village India* (ed. Marriott), Chicago.

R.K.P.C. (1951), *Report of the Kandyan Peasantry Commission*, Colombo.

ROW, T. VENKATASAMI (1883). *A Manual of the District of Tanjore* (2 vols.), Madras.

RYAN, B. (1953), *Caste in Modern Ceylon*, New Brunswick.

SASTRI, K. A. NILAKANDA (1935, 1937), *The Colas* (2 vols.), Madras.

—— (1955), *A History of South India*, Oxford.

SRINIVAS, M. N. (1952), *Religion and Society among the Coorgs of South India*, Oxford.

—— ed. (1955a), *India's Villages*, Bengal.

—— (1955b), 'The Social System of a Mysore Village', in *Village India* (ed. Marriott), Chicago.

—— (1955c), 'Castes: Can they Exist in India of Tomorrow?', in *Economic Weekly*, 15 October 1955, pp. 1231–2, Bombay.

STEIN, SIR AUREL (1929), *On Alexander's Tracks to the Indus*, London.

STEVENSON, H. N. C. (1954), 'Status Evaluation in the Hindu Caste System', in *Journal of the Royal Anthropological Institute*, vol. 84.

TAMBIAH, H. W. (1954), *The Laws and Customs of the Tamils of Ceylon*, Colombo.

TAMBIAH, S. J. (1958), 'The Structure of Kinship and its Relationship to Land Possession and Residence in Pata Dumbara, Central Ceylon', in *Journal of the Royal Anthropological Institute*, vol. 88, part 1, pp. 21–44.

WARNER, W. LLOYD, and LUNT, PAUL S. (1942), *The Status System of a Modern Community*, Yale.

WISER, W. H. (1936), *The Hindu Jajmani System*, Lucknow.

ZIMMER, H. (1946), *Myths and Symbols in Indian Art and Civilization* (ed. J. Campbell), New York.